W9-BKE-483

THIS BOOK IS NO LONGER
THE PROPERTY OF THE
INDIANAPOLIS-MARION COUNTY
PUBLIC LIBRARY

Raymond E. Gnat

Director

PUERTO RICO
Island Between Two Worlds

By the Same Author

America Goes to the Fair
East Africa
Egypt
Ethiopia
Ghana and Ivory Coast
The Global Food Shortage
Mexico

Lila Perl

PUERTO RICO

Island Between Two Worlds

illustrated with photographs

William Morrow and Company · New York · 1979

INDIANAPOLIS MARION CO. PUBLIC LIBRARY

Copyright © 1979 by Lila Perl

All rights reserved. No part of this book may be reproduced or utilized in any form or by any means, electronic or mechanical, including photocopying, recording or by any information storage and retrieval system, without permission in writing from the Publisher. Inquiries should be addressed to William Morrow and Company, Inc., 105 Madison Ave., New York, N. Y. 10016.

Printed in the United States of America
First Edition
1 2 3 4 5 6 7 8 9 10

Library of Congress Cataloging in Publication Data
Perl, Lila.
  Puerto Rico, island between two worlds.

  Bibliography: p.
  Includes index.
  Summary: Examines the history, geography, economy, culture, and politics of Puerto Rico and considers its future as a commonwealth, state, or independent nation.
  1. Puerto Rico—Juvenile literature. [1. Puerto Rico] I. Title.
F1958.3.P47   972.95   79-1130
ISBN 0-688-22181-5
ISBN 0-688-32181-X lib. bdg.

Acknowledgments

The author wishes to express her gratitude to the following for their whole-hearted cooperation and generous assistance:

Doel R. García, Executive Director, Commonwealth of Puerto Rico Tourism Company; Mario E. Benítez, Director of Public Relations; and staff members R. Norris Blake, Olva Mayoral de Abel, Jaime Montilla, and María Julia Marrero; Chancellor Ismael Rodríguez Bou, University of Puerto Rico, Río Piedras; Dr. Belén Serra, Dean of Studies; Dr. Antonio J. Colorado, Advisor, Chancellor's Office; Professor Eladio Rivera Quiñones, Dean, School of Humanities; Dr. Gerardo Navas, Director, Graduate School of Planning; Salvado Tío Montes de Oca, Director, University of Puerto Rico Press; Chancellor Rafael Pietri Oms, University of Puerto Rico, Mayagüez; Tomás Lopez Silva, Director, Alumni Association; Bertram P. Finn-Fernándes, Director, Office of Economic Research, Economic Development Administration; John H. Mudie, Director, Economic Research Department, Government Development Bank for Puerto Rico; Gil Perlroth, Eastern Airlines; Karen Weiner, Hilton International; Andrea Gurvitz, Tromson Monroe, Public Relations; Steven Padilla, Palmasdel Mar; Sister Maureen Wainman; and special thanks for warm and gracious encouragement to Kal Wagenheim.

Deepest appreciation is extended to the following: Jaime Benítez, former United States Resident Commissioner; Rubén Berríos Martínez, President, Puerto Rican Independence Party; Rissig Elwood Licha, Director of Communications for Governor Carlos Romero Barceló, La Fortaleza.

All photographs are by Lila Perl with the exception of the following: Office of Communications, La Fortaleza, page 143; Puerto Rican Independence Party, page 149; United Nations/T. Chen, page 151; United Nations/M. Tzovaras, page 154. Permission is gratefully acknowledged.

K155948

Wrn

Contents

GULF OF
MEXICO

Florida

Key West

BAHAMA
ISLANDS

ATLANTIC OCEAN

N

CUBA

HISPANIOLA

PUERTO
RICO

VIRGIN ISLANDS

MEXICO

HAITI

BRITISH HONDURAS

JAMAICA

DOMINICAN
REPUBLIC

Lesser Antilles

GUATEMALA

Greater Antilles

HONDURAS

EL SALVADOR

CARIBBEAN SEA

NICARAGUA

COSTA RICA

Panama
Canal

PANAMA

PACIFIC OCEAN

COLOMBIA

VENEZUELA

GUIANA

Punta
Borinquén

Isabela

Camuy

Arecibo

Manati

to Desecheo
Island

Aguadilla

RÍO ABAJO
STATE FOREST

Río Camuy

Dos Bocas Lake

Aguada

Rincón

Lares

Utuado

Añasco

Las Marías

Mayagüez

MARICAO
STATE FOREST

Adjuntas

Cerro de Punta 4,389 ft.

CORDILLE
C

San Germán

LAJAS VALLEY

Yauco

Ponce

Boquerón
Beach

Parguera

Guánica

Santa Isa

to Mona
Island

Cabo
Rojo
Lighthouse

Phosphorescent
Bay

Caña Gorda Beach

Puerto Rico
and the West Indies

rado
SAN JUAN
Cataño
Loíza Aldea
Las
Croabas
N
Bayamón
Carolina
Luquillo
Beach
Loíza
Fajardo
to Culebra Island
Río Grande de Loíza
LUQUILLO MOUNTAIN
RANGE
EL YUNQUE
RAIN FOREST
Caguas

arranquitas
to Vieques Island
NTRAL
CAYEY
Humacao
Cayey
MOUNTAIN
Humacao Beach
RANGE
Yabucoa
Maunabo
Culebra Island
Guayama
as
Punta
Guilarte
Beach
Vieques Island

A curving Atlantic beach in the Condado section of San Juan

·I·
Island of the Arawak

In an earlier day, the green and lovely island of Puerto Rico was named La Isla del Encanto, The Isle of Enchantment. Its near-silent shoreline was a succession of sweeping and curving beaches feathered with palm trees, of placid bays and intriguing rocky coves. A short distance inland rose the verdant highlands. The rain forest, in particular, was mysterious and inviting, a lure to the adventurous, not only because of the incredible size and lushness of its plant life but because it was reportedly inhabited by the spirits of the long-vanished Taino Indians, members of the widespread Arawakan family.

Today much of Puerto Rico's natural beauty has been altered by the features of modern industrial life. Ribbons of auto roads encircle the island and crisscross the interior. Former farmlands near the coastal plain are overrun with single-family housing developments and vast shopping malls. High-rise condominiums, intermingled with a lesser number of sleek tourist hotels, accent the sandy ocean shores. And the hushed mountain glens are pockmarked with the graveyards of mangled and rusting automobiles.

Yet much of the scenic appeal of this tropical island is still evident, and there is a growing awareness of the ecological and aesthetic damage wrought by the rapid social and economic changes of the past few decades. It is not too late, perhaps, for Puerto Rico to regain its place as one of the most diversely beautiful islands of the Caribbean.

Like its neighbor islands, all of which are part of the curving chain of the West Indies, Puerto Rico was born out of a giant, prehistoric upheaval of the earth's crust. The three large clusters comprising the West Indies are the Bahama Islands, which lie entirely in the Atlantic, the Greater Antilles, and the Lesser Antilles, both groups

11

lying mainly or entirely in the Caribbean. All of these scattered bits of land, some fairly large, others tiny, are really the peaks of a great mountain chain that once linked North and South America. Today most of that once-rugged landmass is a sunken plain beneath the Caribbean Sea.

When Columbus first approached these "Indies" of the West, he still assumed that they were the gateway to the mainland of India, and so he named them the Antilles, meaning "preceding" or "before." The four largest islands came to be known as the Greater Antilles, while the groups of smaller ones curving for 600 miles or more southward to Venezuela were named the Lesser Antilles.

Of the Greater Antilles, Puerto Rico is the smallest and most easterly. Cuba, 500 miles to the west, is the largest. In between lie Hispaniola, today shared by the countries of Haiti and the Dominican Republic, and Jamaica, which is next smallest after Puerto Rico. Puerto Rico is the only one of the Greater Antillean islands that is not, and has never been, an independent nation.

The Antilles, Greater and Lesser, appear on the map as a series of dashes and dots forming a northern and eastern boundary that boxes in the Caribbean waters. So the northern coast of Puerto Rico is washed by the surf of the Atlantic Ocean, while the gentler Caribbean bathes its southern shore. The same is true for the islands of Cuba and Hispaniola. So deeply fissured is the Atlantic floor in this part of the world that only a couple of miles off the northwest coast of Puerto Rico the sea begins to deepen considerably. At about fifty miles north of Puerto Rico, the Atlantic bottoms into a chasm some 29,000 feet deep, known as the Milwaukee Depth. If measured from the floor of this undersea abyss, Puerto Rico's highest mountains, which are only about 4,000 feet tall, would be some 33,000 feet high, exceeding the highest peaks of the Himalayas.

Puerto Rico is a rectangular body of land, measuring about 100 miles from east to west and only about 35 miles from north to south. Including its offshore islands, its total area is only 3,435 square miles. Probably an easy way to visualize the size and contour of Puerto Rico is to think of a slightly altered Long Island, similar in length but roughly doubled in thickness. This doubling would make Long Island just about as wide from north to south as Puerto Rico and would make it approximately equal to Puerto Rico in land area.

But the climate and topography of the two are, of course, very different, for Puerto Rico lies 1,662 miles southeast of New York (and over 1,000 miles southeast of Miami). Its extreme easterly position puts it on Atlantic Standard Time, which is one hour later than the Eastern Standard Time of the United States.

Partly because of its geographical location, Puerto Rico has long occupied a pivotal position between North and South America, between the different cultural worlds of the Atlantic and the Caribbean. Also, beginning with the voyages of Columbus, the island became a gateway, a key point along the east-west shipping routes between the Old World and the New.

The two most prominent physical features of Puerto Rico are its narrow, encircling coastal plain and its extensive mountainous interior. The principal mountain range is the Cordillera Central, an east-west spine that runs about two-thirds of the island's length and bisects it into a moister northern half and a drier southern half. The

Inland mountains that loom beyond the built-up coastal plain

island's highest point, the Cerro de Punta rises 4,389 feet and lies almost at its geographical center.

Other mountainous spurs of substantial size are the Maricao State Forest of the southwestern quarter of the island, the Río Abajo State Forest of the northwestern region, the Cayey Mountain Range in the southeast, and the Luquillo Mountain Range in the northeast. At Luquillo's eastern extremity is the famous El Yunque Rain Forest. It is named for its 3,496-foot peak, which is shaped like an anvil, or *yunque* in Spanish. But two slightly taller peaks in this moist, dripping forest exceed 3,500 feet.

The rain forest is aptly named for it receives the greatest amount of rainfall in all of Puerto Rico, 180 to 200 inches a year. This phenomenon is due to the prevailing winds from the northeast, which blow diagonally across the island, bending and shaping the palms on its northern and eastern beaches. As the humid trade winds sweep in from the Atlantic and across the narrow coastal plain they abruptly encounter the easterly heights of the Luquillo Range. The air rises, cools, and condenses into rain. From a sunny coastal point, such as the exquisite palm-shaded crescent of Luquillo Beach, a blue-gray haze surrounds El Yunque and the two higher peaks, Mount Britton and El Toro, which are often shrouded in cloud.

The rain forest is a magical world of giant tree ferns, growing twenty and thirty feet high on thick, woody, trunks; of enormous clumps of sturdy bamboo vaulting fifty feet toward the heavens. Gnarled, woody vines called "lianas" loop themselves from tree to tree searching for sunlight, while epiphytes, or air plants, nest like birds in the branches of tall trees, thriving on the water they trap in their leaves or in their dangling fleshy roots. Although these oddly perched plants, which include bromeliads with spiky, pineapplelike leaves and certain varieties of orchids, appear to be parasites, they are not, for they do not live off their hosts.

Everywhere in the forest lie the large, fallen leaves of the *yagrumo* tree. Deeply notched, they curl inward as they dry, exposing their silvery undersides. Puerto Ricans say that a two-faced person is *"yagrumo,"* because like the leaf of this tree—deep-green on top, pale-green on bottom—there are two sides to his (or her) character.

14

The dramatic palm-fringed crescent of Luquillo Beach

Officially this mountain preserve is known as the Caribbean National Forest. It is administered by the United States Forest Service and is the only tropical forest in the entire system, which extends to Puerto Rico because of the island's commonwealth relationship with the United States. Just beyond the Visitor Center, which is located at about 2,000 feet of elevation, foot trails take off for the 3,500-foot

Coca Falls in the El Yunque Rain Forest

peaks. As one ascends, the character of the vegetation changes from that of rain forest to montane thicket, to sierra palm, and ultimately to moss-draped dwarf forest—a total of four different ecosystems that have developed in response to increased elevations and the accompanying temperature changes.

16

Birds are plentiful in the rain forest, and it is even possible to catch a glimpse of the almost extinct Puerto Rican parrot, found nowhere else on the island. Most audible, although almost impossible to spot, is the tiny, thumbnail-size tree frog known as the *coqui*. Believed to be unique to Puerto Rico, the beloved *coqui* produces a sweet, clear, two-note call—*ko-kee'*—which is more birdlike than froglike and from which it takes its name. Throughout the island the *coqui* can be heard "singing" in shrubbery and other damp outdoor places soon after sundown and often into the dawn. But in the rain forest a chorus of *coquis* chirps incessantly day and night.

The driest region of Puerto Rico lies diagonally opposite the rain forest, on the southwest coast. Emptied of their moisture by a succession of mountain ranges, the last of which is the Maricao State Forest, the northeast winds bring as little as ten inches of rainfall a year to parts of this area. The parched-looking landscape is semi-desert in places, and, just as in the southwestern United States, cactus and chaparral growth—scrubby, thorny, dwarfed vegetation—are found here. Also present are the tamarind tree, with its fleshy, oblong brown pods that are crushed into a sweetened, acidy paste or drink, and the kapok, or "silk-cotton" tree. The fine, light fibers that are found in the seed pods of the kapok tree are suitable for mattress and pillow stuffing.

The Lajas Valley in this region is good cropland but requires artificial irrigation. In the vicinity of the Cabo Rojo lighthouse, at the extreme southwesterly tip of Puerto Rico, salt is evaporated from the sea. The sun glares down on the shimmering salt flats, the air is hot and still, and the wind-rustled palms and vigorous surf of the northern coast seem far more than a mere thirty-five miles away.

Still another distinctive feature of the Puerto Rican landscape are the karst, or limestone, formations that cover large areas of the north central and northwestern regions. The numerous "haystacks" and sinkholes—large, knobby hillocks and deep, craterlike pits—are the result of the prolonged action of water on soluble elements in the layers of limestone rock. Unlike the bare limestone hills of western Yugoslavia (where the word *karst* originates), those of warm, humid

Salt flats near Cabo Rojo lighthouse in the dry,
southwestern corner of the island

Karst hills on the horizon in the Río Abajo State Forest

Puerto Rico are covered with thick vegetation and show few out-croppings of naked rock. They bulge like gigantic, furry green pimples on the landscape of the flat coastal plain and form scalloped horizons as they climb the slopes of the Río Abajo State Forest. The limestone craters of the karst country provide a sinister note. They often measure several hundred feet across, and some are deep enough to hold a twenty-story building. From the precarious rim of such a pit it appears deceptively shallow, filled with low-growing shrubs. In actuality these are the leafy tops of very tall trees.

Puerto Rico's karst region has proved the ideal setting for the Arecibo Ionospheric Observatory. The existence of an enormous 300-foot-deep sinkhole, over 1300 feet in diameter, lessened the cost of excavating a massive pit and served for the installation of the ob-servatory's huge aluminum reflector plate. Via the world's largest radar-radio telescope, pulses are transmitted and received that tell us a great deal about our solar system and distant galaxies. The ob-servatory is operated by Cornell University for the National Science Foundation of the United States.

Surface caves and extensive underground caverns are also present in Puerto Rico's karst country. A fairly recent tracing of the disap-pearing Camuy River, which abruptly vanishes underground, has re-vealed that the river emerges on the floor of a vast and, as yet, little-explored cave system believed to be among the largest in the world.

Many short rivers, which flood their banks in the rainy season, gush seaward from the Puerto Rican highlands. None, however, is longer than fifty miles. The island's rivers are navigable to small craft only. At the coastal village of Loíza Aldea, to the east of the capital of San Juan, the Río Grande de Loíza makes its way into the Atlantic. As no bridge has been built across the stream, cars and trucks are ferried across, up to four at a time, on a raft that is hauled by ropes. Puerto Rico's lakes, such as the majestically set, fork-shaped Dos Bocas Lake in the Río Abajo State Forest, are man-made, the result of damming the island's rushing waterways to provide hydroelectric power.

The waters surrounding Puerto Rico are dotted with a number of

19

islands. To the east lie the two major offshore islands of Vieques (nine miles from the coast and measuring about fifty-two square miles in area) and Culebra (twenty-two miles away and measuring only seven miles in length and four miles in width). The populations of the two are small and engage mainly in fishing and agriculture. In addition to table fish, the surrounding waters contain dolphin, the manatee, or sea cow, and a variety of sea turtles.

Not unlike the industrial pollution that has altered the quality of life on parts of the main island, Vieques and Culebra have undergone several decades of noise pollution due to United States naval operations that have included ship-to-shore target practice and aerial gunnery. Damage has also occurred to the islands' coral reefs and other marine life due to pollution of the waters through shelling and warship activity.

Beyond Vieques and Culebra lie the United States Virgin Islands, about forty miles from the coast of Puerto Rico. They are its nearest neighbor on the east. Smaller islands close to the northeastern coast are Icacos and Palominos, used as camping and recreation destinations. Ferries and private boats leave for the larger and smaller easterly islands from the busy coastal town of Fajardo.

Just over forty miles off Puerto Rico's southwestern coast is Mona Island, about twenty square miles in area and lying in the channel of the same name. Mona is located roughly halfway between Puerto Rico and the Dominican Republic, Puerto Rico's nearest neighbor on the west. The Mona Channel, or Passage, is an international north-south shipping route between the Atlantic and the Caribbean. Like tiny Desecheo Island, which lies closer in off Puerto Rico's northwesterly shore, Mona Island is uninhabited. It is a haven for wild goats, wild pigs, and iguanas, and it is occasionally visited by hunters.

Off Puerto Rico's southern coast, near the town of Parguera, lies the famed Phosphorescent Bay, a calm mangrove-fringed inlet in which an unusual concentration of tiny, luminescent organisms thrives. These single-celled, microscopic creatures are known as dinoflagellates because of their ability to propel themselves through the water with two tiny whiplike extremities. So great are their numbers here that the movement of a boat entering the bay on a moonless night reveals flashes of silver light leaping and zigzagging through the dark waters. The streaks, caused by the movement of fish, may be several feet long and inches wide. The wake of the fast-moving boat is a bluish foam that gives off an eerie glow, and a scooped-up pail of water brought on board is brilliant with confettilike sparkles as one flicks fingers through it. Water splashed on the deck dances briefly with points of light.

While bioluminescent organisms are not unusual in themselves, their density in this Puerto Rican habitat is, and steps are being taken to protect the bay from pollution and from distant shore lights that might destroy or dim this rare phenomenon of nature.

The mangrove swamps of the Parguera coastal region, and of parts of the northern coast, are thick, islandlike clusters of vegetation. They are formed as the trees, which thrive in calm salt water, put forth branches that become stiltlike roots, advancing slowly to reclaim land from the sea.

Traveling eastward toward Ponce, Puerto Rico's second largest city (with a population of over 150,000), the unspoiled southern coast gives way to a scene of heavy industrialization. Oil refineries, petrochemical plants, and cement works spew smoke, stench, and dust into the air. Stemming mainly from the economic development phase of the late 1960's, these environment-polluting operations have also affected the beaches, the water, and the soil, and they have considerably altered the quality of life in an area that was once devoted to sugarcane cultivation. Pollution is also a serious problem on Puerto Rico's northern coast, in the vicinity of San Juan, where a population of over one million is concentrated and where, at certain shore points, both sanitary and storm sewers empty into the ocean along recreational beaches used by the public.

Despite its hundreds of miles of seacoast, Puerto Rico does not have a well-developed fishing industry. In part, this lack is due to the extreme depth of the surrounding waters, which makes commercial fishing impractical. Deep-sea sport fishermen, however, catch marlin, sailfish, dolphin, barracuda, and mackerel in these waters.

Oddly enough, one of the most popular fish in the Puerto Rican

21

diet is bacalao, dried, salted cod, caught off the Newfoundland banks and introduced to the island in colonial times by the Spanish, among whom it has been a staple for centuries. Nor does the tuna that is canned in modern factories in and around the city of Mayagüez come from local waters. It is caught off the west coast of South America, often as far away as the Galápagos Islands, and is shipped via the Panama Canal to Puerto Rico for processing.

While there are daily local catches of fresh fish such as red snapper (*chillo*), shrimp, and lobster, these varieties are apt to be found mainly in small fishing communities like Rincón, Boquerón, Parguera, and Las Croabas. Residents of San Juan and other towns are likely to buy supermarket packages of frozen fish caught in distant places and processed and marketed by giant American food corporations.

A worthy effort to increase the consumption of fresh fish among Puerto Ricans, and at the same time to encourage freshwater game fishing, is being made by the Puerto Rican Department of Agriculture, which has stocked the rivers, ponds, lagoons, canals, and manmade lakes with nonindigenous table fish that adapt well to the environment. Experiments with new varieties are conducted at the fish hatchery in the Maricao State Forest, which has already introduced an abundance of edible fish such as widemouth bass, sunfish, and catfish from the United States and tilapia from Africa.

Among the island's wildlife there are no large or fierce animals. Land crabs, which are plentiful in shore areas, are caught and strung together for sale along the coastal roads. Known as *jueyes,* or *cangrejos,* they are eaten boiled or made into a tasty filling for crisp, fried pastry turnovers and other snack foods. The iguana is not found in inhabited areas, but tiny lizards scurry around on walks and garden walls. The snake population has been reduced by the presence of the mongoose, introduced from India, and bothersome insects are surprisingly rare.

Flowering shrubs and trees adorn the island with vibrant hues of flame red, canary yellow, hot pink, and deep purple, as well as lavender and creamy white. Among the most commonly seen blossoms

22

Live land crabs for sale at a roadside stand

An iguana, still to be found on the uninhabited offshore islands

are those of the tulip tree, oleander, bougainvillea (called *trinitaria* in Puerto Rico), hibiscus, jacaranda, and frangipani. Most flamboyant is the aptly named *flamboyán* tree, which is cloaked in a mass of brick-red blooms during the spring and summer months. It is more widely known as the royal poinciana.

Although warm throughout the year, with temperatures ranging daily from a low of about seventy degrees Fahrenheit to a high of about eighty-five, the Puerto Rican climate is not oppressive due to the steadily flowing trade winds. In summer, and occasionally even in February and March, a daily high may run up into the low nineties. At higher elevations, however, nighttime readings may drop into the fifties and even the forties.

Rain falls all year, but in brief, local showers so that almost every day has long periods of sunshine. Rain is more likely between May and November, but it varies with location. San Juan, on the north side of the island, receives sixty inches of rainfall compared with thirty to forty inches at Ponce on the drier south side.

From time to time hurricanes have hit the island and caused great destruction. Since 1508, when records were first kept, there have been more than seventy, and they were surely known to the Taino Indians, who named them for the evil god, Juracán, who darkened the skies and brought the terrifying gale winds. The English word *hurricane* is derived from the Taino language.

The severest storms of the past hundred years have been San Ciriaco in 1899, San Felipe in 1928, and San Ciprián in 1932. The first two devastated the coffee-growing zones and nearly annihilated that branch of Puerto Rican agriculture, while the third attacked the San Juan urban area. All caused numerous deaths and injuries and widespread homelessness.

Since the United States Weather Service has taken over, the practice of naming hurricanes after saints' days falling close to the time of the disaster has been discontinued. Instead, the Weather Service has been identifying hurricanes with the names of women, in order of alphabetical appearance each season (a practice now being held up to scrutiny for its sexist implications). Donna, in 1960, was responsible for a loss of eighty lives, and Eloise in 1975 caused severe flooding and resulted in thirty-four deaths. Most hurricanes have occurred in August or September.

Earthquakes are not a serious threat to Puerto Rico, although small tremors do occur because of the volcanic nature of parts of the undersea Caribbean plain.

The mineral resource that drew the sixteenth-century explorers to the New World was, of course, gold. The placer-mined streams of Puerto Rico were soon exhausted, but the island also has some manganese, iron, cobalt, nickel, and titanium. Rich copper deposits exist in the Cordillera Central, in the triangle formed by the towns of Lares, Utuado, and Adjuntas. So far their exploitation by foreign companies has been fought by environmentalists and proindependence groups. The sharp drop in the price of world copper since 1974, and Puerto Rico's awareness of the damage wrought by its foreign-owned refineries and petrochemical plants, make intensive mining of the island's copper unlikely in the very near future.

Nonmetals such as silica sands, clay, gravel, limestone, and marble are quite abundant. They are used for building materials and are processed commercially into glass containers, ceramics, cement, and concrete. Puerto Rico's virgin forests once yielded woods for building and for making charcoal, which was the principal cooking fuel. Today the valuable *ausubo* tree, from which the first houses of the Spanish settlement were constructed, is almost extinct in Puerto Rico. Other tropical trees, including a number of hardwood varieties, are being preserved or planted in reforestation programs to prevent mud slides and soil erosion.

So little is known about the earliest human inhabitants of Puerto Rico that they have been labeled simply the Arcaicos, or Archaics. They are believed to have come from the North American mainland, probably Florida, and to have reached the island via Cuba, traveling on crude rafts of lashed-together logs. The first groups may have arrived anytime between 20,000 and 5,000 years ago, but their culture was so primitive that no clear-cut signs of it are left to us. There has been some speculation that the Archaics were responsible for cave drawings found on Mona Island and for flints discovered near Cabo Rojo. In any case, they were apparently a fishing and food-gathering people who were able to draw sustenance from the tropical vegetation and marine life of the island without having to till the soil.

The Archaics were followed by a much more advanced group, members of the Arawak language family known as the Igneri Indians. Arawakan peoples inhabited northern South America—the region that extends from coastal Brazil through Venezuela to Colombia—and made their way north by island-hopping along the Lesser Antilles chain. They are believed to have reached Puerto Rico at about the time of Christ, perhaps a couple of hundred years earlier. They were farmers, and introduced corn and tobacco to the island. Their artifacts, now displayed in Puerto Rican museums, include household tools, articles of body adornment, ceremonial objects, and pottery decorated in red and white. The Igneri appear to have had a settlement near Loíza Aldea, where land crabs were plentiful and formed an important part of their diet. A dig at that site has actually produced the skeletal remains of an Igneri man believed to have lived between A.D. 300 and 700. The find has been placed in the Adolfo de Hostos Museum in Old San Juan, the historic quarter of the island's capital.

Best known to us is the last major Indian group to appear, the Tainos, who were also of the Arawak family. From their arrival in about A.D. 1000 to the early 1500's, when the first Europeans began their settlement, the Tainos' culture and society dominated the island, which they called Boriquén, or Land of the Noble Lord. Not only were the Tainos most advanced in their intricate carvings in stone, wood, and clay, in their shellwork and goldwork, they were organized into a stratified social structure and enjoyed a stable, civilized, and peaceful existence.

Although the Tainos fashioned gold ornaments from nuggets found in the riverbeds, they were a Stone Age people to whom metal weapons were unknown. When harassed by their fierce neighbors from other islands, the Caribs, they used stone axes or arrows tipped with sharpened bone or shell to defend themselves. The Caribs, who had also originated in South America, were members of the Cariban language family, and it is from them that the Caribbean Sea takes its name. They were reported to be aggressive, ferocious, and cannibalistic.

In appearance, the Tainos were copper-skinned, had dark, straight hair, and were short by present-day standards. Like the Mayans of Mexico and Central America, they admired a sloping forehead and bound their infants' heads with cotton bands to achieve this effect. Their homes, which were called *bohios*, were neat, circular huts built of poles of bamboo or sapling and roofed with palm or other thatch. The dwellings were raised up on posts, slightly above ground, to keep them from being flooded during periods of heavy rainfall. Usually they contained a stone bench and a crude fireplace, vessels of clay pottery, and finely woven baskets. Hammocks, popular in Puerto Rico to this day, were used for sleeping or lounging and could be folded up and put away when not in use. The very name for this space-saving type of bed comes from the Taino word *hamaca*.

Taino life depicted in an exhibit at the
Dominican Convent in Old San Juan

The *bohíos* were clustered in villages, each of which had its own cacique, or chief. His house, usually rectangular and with a veranda, was the most prominent and faced on the village square, or main plaza, just as the *alcaldía*, or city hall, does in Puerto Rican towns today. The plaza was called the *batey* and was used for meetings, military drill, and other local functions.

Clothing was made of cotton, which grew wild and was also cultivated. The principal garment was the *nagua,* a short, sheathlike wrap that was worn by married women. The Spanish word, *enaguas,* meaning petticoat or underskirt, derives from this Taino word. Fibers for fishing nets and hammocks came from cactus or other fibrous-leaved plants. Body ornaments included necklaces and leg and arm bracelets of animal teeth, bone, shell, and stones. The chiefs wore feather headdresses and gold neck pendants.

Body paint and textile dyes were derived from plants, particularly *achiote* berries, which are the seeds of the annatto tree and impart a vivid yellow-orange hue. *Achiote* is a popular coloring and flavoring substance in Puerto Rico today. The berries, lightly cooked in oil, produce an extract, which can be combined with rice. The deep golden color substitutes for that of saffron, a costly spice which is called for in certain Spanish dishes that appear often in the Puerto Rican cuisine.

The food staple of the Tainos was the cassava, the tuberous root of a leafy shrub native to South America. Boiled cassava is bland, white, and starchy, and it tastes something like a slippery boiled potato. Corn was also grown by the Tainos, but did not do so well on the moist tropical island and could be cultivated only on its drier southern half. Beans of several varieties, originating in South and Central America, and vegetables of the squash family formed the remainder of the edible crops that were grown. To cultivate them, and their cotton and tobacco, the Tainos used crude agricultural tools that consisted mainly of digging sticks.

The Taino diet was rounded out with crabs, clams, and sea turtles that were snared when they came ashore to lay their eggs. River fish were caught with nets or by spearing them with a narcotic substance

28

extracted from plants, and some sea fishing was done from canoes. The iguana and other small animals, wild birds, and dogs that were domesticated and fattened for the table, provided meat.

A variety of tropical fruits grew wild—the papaya, the guava, and the pineapple. Others, rarer but still found in parts of the island today, included the *nispero*, the brown-skinned, tan-fleshed fruit of the sapodilla, or chicle tree, the *acerola*, a small, cherrylike fruit, and the mamey, or mammee-apple, a fruit with juicy yellow pulp that is not an apple at all.

Most of the many starchy tubers that are so popular in today's Puerto Rican diet were brought there by its African population, and its bananas, plantains, sugarcane, coconut, oranges, mangoes, rice, and breadfruit all have their origins in Asia or the Pacific. Many of these foods were introduced by the European explorers, who also brought horses, goats, pigs, cattle, and poultry to the island.

The Taino religion centered on a supreme being and creator called Yukiyú. He was presumably the Noble Lord for whom the island of Boriquén was named, and his dwelling place was believed to be somewhere in the misty heights of the rain forest. Juracán, the evil god who brought the hurricanes and other disasters, was the devil who opposed and threatened Yukiyú. A body of priests acted as intermediaries between the people and these two powerful beings. They also gave advice on spiritual matters and dispensed cures for illness.

In their own homes and villages, the people kept images of lesser gods or protective spirits known as *cemis*. They were small, carved heads of stone, wood, or clay. Only one large *cemi*, the crouched body of a man carved in stone and weighing over 200 pounds, has been found so far, in the Dominican Republic. The Tainos believed that after death the spirits of the departed went to live in the remote mountain heights of the island, possibly in the rain-forest realm of the god Yukiyú. The spirits were said to rest by day and occasionally to visit the living by night. This belief led to the village practice of leaving an offering of food in the *bohío* before retiring, to be eaten by the shades of the deceased.

Little is known about the public religious ceremonies of the

Stone *cemis*, the household gods of the Tainos, on display
in the Museum of the University of Puerto Rico

Tainos, and the mystery has deepened in many ways since the excavation in the 1950's of the Indian Ceremonial Ball Park located near the mountain town of Utuado. This center, which dates back to A.D. 1200 and is believed to have been of combined religious and recreational significance, consists of a number of stone-bordered plazas, or playing fields, one round and all the rest rectangular. The largest plaza is edged with upright monoliths of granite, some of which are engraved with tracings of human figures and one with that of a bird.

The ball game, which is almost certainly related to a similar one known in the Mayan culture, was probably played by two teams of anywhere from ten to thirty men. The ball, which is reported by early Spanish observers to have bounced, may have been of a rubber-like substance. It was hit only with the head, shoulders, elbows, hips, or knees—never the hands—much as in the modern game of soccer. Handsomely carved stone collars or rings have been excavated at the site, but their purpose has never been determined. Might they have been hoops through which the ball had to pass, and, if so, where and how were they affixed? How was the game scored, and what was its connection with the Taino religion? Why was the ball park lo-

Decorated stones bordering the large plaza at the Indian
Ceremonial Ball Park near Utuado

cated at such a distance from most of the Taino centers of population, which were in the coastal region?

Researchers tell us that teams of women, too, played the ceremonial ball game of the Tainos. This custom is not surprising when
we learn that their society was matriarchal. The village chiefs, and
also the grand cacique who ruled over the entire island, all inherited
their positions of absolute power through the female line. When a
cacique died, the son of his sister, rather than his own son, took his
place. Not only did women occupy a dominant position in the family,

31

they had many legal rights equal with those of men, including the ownership of property. The Spanish reported the existence of at least one female ruler, the "caciqua" Loíza.

Beginning early in the sixteenth century the Indian population, which was believed to have numbered 30,000 to 40,000 at the time of Columbus, succumbed rapidly to the military superiority of the Spanish conquistadors. In a mere twenty years, the island's Taino inhabitants had been drastically reduced to an estimated 4,000. And probably not long afterward the last pure-blooded Taino ceased to exist on Boriquén.

Today, as part of their pride in their Indian roots, Puerto Ricans like to point out the places on the island that take their names from their Taino forebears, such as the city of Mayagüez and the towns of Arecibo, Caguas, Yauco, and Humacao. And, occasionally a Puerto Rican face will stand out from the crowd with features seeming to bespeak a strong Indian heritage.

Probably most significant among the Taino contributions has been the island's name, Boriquén (which, through an early Spanish mispronunciation, is often written Borinquén). To Puerto Ricans, the word Boriquén is synonymous with their cultural identity. And not surprisingly the Puerto Rican "national" anthem is called "La Borinqueña."

Yet no matter how much Puerto Ricans may think of themselves as a "nation," they are not, in fact, a sovereign people. Unlike many of their West Indian neighbors, they are still searching today for a clear-cut political identity. At the same time, Puerto Ricans do share a heritage with a number of other Caribbean peoples whose Indian forebears have all but vanished and whose ethnic makeup was ordained centuries ago by the colonial ambitions and expediencies of far-off Spain.

·II·
Colony to Commonwealth

Christopher Columbus, on his first voyage to America in 1492, must have sailed quite close to the island of Puerto Rico. Yet he had no inkling of its existence. After stopping at the Bahamas and Cuba and leaving a small settlement on the northern coast of Hispaniola, he set a northeasterly course toward home, possibly missing the coast of Boriquén by a mere hundred miles.

Returning to the West Indies on his second voyage in 1493, Columbus commanded a fleet much larger than the three small vessels of his first journey. He now had seventeen ships that carried a crew and passengers of 1,200, including artisans, laborers, astronomers, and mapmakers. There were no women among the would-be colonists.

This time the route followed across the Atlantic was more southerly, and the first islands sighted by the expedition were those of the Lesser Antilles. The fleet then sailed northward along the curving land chain, heading for Hispaniola. On an island that Columbus christened Santa María de Guadalupe (now Guadeloupe), a small group of Indians from the island of Boriquén asked to be taken aboard and returned to their home. They had been captured and transported by the warlike Carib Indians, who lived scattered among the Lesser Antilles and often raided the Greater Antillean home of the Tainos.

After passing the Virgin Islands and the offshore island of Vieques, the ship carrying the Tainos came in sight of the eastern coast of the main island, at which point the Tainos jumped overboard and swam ashore. Columbus sailed on along the southern coast of Boriquén and up the west coast, finally dropping anchor in a suitable bay in order to take on fresh water, food, and wood for fuel.

The statue of Columbus in the Plaza de Colón in Old San Juan

His exact landing point is uncertain to this day, but the town of Aguada has laid claim to it with a white stone marker topped with a cross. As Columbus never set foot on the North American mainland, Puerto Rico prides itself on being the only bit of United States territory visited by the great discoverer. The landing took place on

November 19, 1493, a date that is celebrated annually in Puerto Rico as Discovery Day. In 1893, on the 400th anniversary of the landing, a statue of Columbus was erected in a prominent plaza in Old San Juan.

After bestowing the Christian name of San Juan Bautista (Saint John the Baptist) on the island of Boriquén, Columbus sailed on to Hispaniola. Although the settlement of the previous year had been wiped out and no Europeans had survived, a new settlement was soon established. During Columbus's third and fourth voyages to America, Hispaniola remained the center of Spain's colonial administration in the West Indies. Its seat of government, Santo Domingo (originally called Nueva Isabela), which was established on the southern coast in 1496, became the oldest European-founded city in the western hemisphere.

The nearby island of San Juan Bautista was largely ignored until after the death of Columbus in 1506. Earlier, two Spanish explorers had been authorized to set up a colony there, but neither had shown any particular interest in doing so. In 1508, however, the explorer Juan Ponce de León, who had been with Columbus on his voyage of 1493, took advantage of the permission to colonize granted him by Nicolás de Ovando, Governor-General of the Spanish West Indies.

Ponce de León sailed from Santo Domingo with fifty men and landed on the southern coast of San Juan de Bautista, where he was received by the grand cacique, Agüeybana the Elder. In a ritual that was designed to express brotherhood, the two exchanged names. The Spanish then proceeded to the northern coast and chose a site for a fortified settlement at Caparra, a couple of miles south of San Juan Bay.

Today Caparra is part of sprawling metropolitan San Juan and lies about midway between the city's section of Santurce and the outlying municipality of Bayamón. The stone foundations of the stronghouse, an official dwelling and headquarters built by Ponce de León, were unearthed in 1936, and a museum just in back of them holds artifacts of the Taino culture as well as fragments of early Spanish life found at the excavation—Spanish-manufactured tiles that adorned the house, furniture hardware, metal tools and weapons, and items of Spanish military dress.

In the following year, 1509, Ponce de León was named governor of San Juan Bautista. Caparra, however, proved to be a poor choice for the capital. It was swampy, insect-infested, and too far from the harbor. And so plans were made to move the seat of government to the north side of San Juan Bay, onto a spit of land that was to become the walled enclave today known as Old San Juan. So magnificent was its natural harbor, well protected from the pounding surf of the nearby Atlantic, that this new site and point of entry to the island was termed a *puerto rico*, or rich port. Then, possibly through a mapmaker's misunderstanding, an odd thing happened. The names of the island and of the new settlement got switched around; the capital city became San Juan, while the island became Puerto Rico. They have remained so to this day.

Ponce de León did not remain on the island. In 1513, he journeyed to Florida in search of the legendary Fountain of Youth and stayed

Ponce de León statue in the Plaza de San José, with the church of the same name in the background

away until 1515. On his second expedition to Florida, in 1521, he was mortally wounded in a fight with the Indians and was brought to Cuba, where he soon died of his injuries. He never lived in the handsomely situated Casa Blanca in Old San Juan, which was built by his family in the year of his death. Eventually, however, his body was returned to Puerto Rico, which has claimed this first Spanish governor as its own. From 1559, his remains lay in the San José Church; in 1908, they were removed to a marble tomb in the San Juan Cathedral. One of the longest streets in modern San Juan is named for him, as is the city of Ponce on the south coast.

The principal lure of Puerto Rico for the Spanish colonists was, of course, its gold. Stream beds, like that of the Río Grande de Loíza, actually produced gold nuggets. By 1510, the first smelted gold was being sent to Spain. The following year, in recognition of the colony's dutiful contribution of the "king's fifth," Ferdinand of Spain granted Puerto Rico its seal, or coat-of-arms.

The colony was grateful for this royal tribute, one of the first coats-of-arms assigned to a territory in the New World. In the inner panel of the seal, a lamb, representing Jesus Christ and bearing a white flag of peace, rests on a Holy Bible. Surrounding this central design is an outer panel, which bears the several symbols of the kingdom of Castile and those Spanish royal houses joined to it as well as the cross of Jerusalem, representing Catholic authority. Although Puerto Rico ceased to be a colony of Spain in 1898, it still displays this emblem bestowed in the year 1511.

No sooner had the seal been granted, however, than it became evident that the island's gold reserves were limited. The stream-mined gold began to run out, and the Indians were put to work digging for rich mother lodes in the mountains. But the sources that supplied the riverbeds soon proved to be sparse. At about the same time, the Indians began a series of rebellions.

With the arrival of the first Spanish settlers, radical changes had taken place in the lives of the Taínos. At first, the Indians were awed by the horses, armor, metal tools, and noisily fired weapons of the almost "godlike" Spaniards, and they met their demands for porters

37

The seal of Puerto Rico on a plaque in the Dominican Convent

and laborers. But very soon came the abuses of the *repartimiento,* a system of "distribution" under which the Indians were rounded up for labor brigades and assigned to the building of Spanish forts and residences or put to work in the mines and in the fields. A similar institution was the *encomienda,* or "commandery," under which the Tainos were taken from their villages and made to live and work on a landed estate under a *patrón,* who was also entrusted with teaching them the Christian religion and Spanish cultural traditions. The *repartimiento* and the *encomienda* were devices that imposed forced labor and serfhood on the Indians. And although the Spanish crown recommended that liberalizing reforms should be instituted, Spain was thousands of miles away and the colonists had an immediate, pressing need for a work force on the island.

By 1510, two years after the landing of Ponce de León, the Indians had succeeded in demolishing the myth that the Spanish "gods" were immortal. A Spanish colonist, Diego Salcedo, traveling in the west coast region of the cacique Urayoán in the company of Indian guides and porters, was put to death by drowning as he crossed the Río Grande de Añasco. After waiting several days on the riverbank beside Salcedo's lifeless body, to make sure that he would not be revived through divine intervention, the Tainos gained the courage to rebel against their Spanish masters.

There followed a series of attacks on the colonists, which were met with harsh retaliation. In one of the counterattacks, Agüeybana II, known as the Brave, was killed. He had succeeded his uncle, Agüeybana the Elder, as grand cacique, and his death severely demoralized the Tainos. The Indians realized that despite their superior numbers they were doomed by the weaponry of the Europeans, and they began to flee into the mountains of the interior or to set out in small boats for neighboring islands. Many simply committed suicide with their families.

Bartolomé de las Casas, the Spanish missionary who had first arrived in the West Indies in 1502, wrote at length of the mistreatment of the Indians in Puerto Rico and elsewhere in the New World. But his words had little effect. And, because of the rapidly dwindling Taino population and the growing demand for labor, the first African slaves began to be brought to the island.

Blacks had appeared on Boriquén as early as 1509, for there were a number of freemen as well as hired servants of African origin who had accompanied the Spaniards on their various expeditions to the West Indies. Not until 1518, however, did the first Portuguese slave ships begin to arrive. With the establishment in the 1520's of the first sugar plantations in the vicinity of San Germán, the second town to be built on the island, the need for field labor increased. Unfortunately, there was no las Casas to protest the status and treatment of the Africans. Black slavery was widely accepted in the world of the sixteenth century and, in fact, was far more prevalent on other islands of the Caribbean, including those colonized by the French and the British, where there was more level land available for sugarcane cultivation and production was much more intensive.

For a time, especially after the gold supply was exhausted around 1530, it was hoped that sugar would boost Puerto Rico's failing economy. Sugar mills for crushing the cane and extracting the juice were built, and new landholders arrived from Spain. But the longed-for riches did not roll in. Meantime, the wealthy Inca empire had been discovered and conquered in Peru. The sugar planters of Puerto Rico thought longingly of the gold of South America and silently prayed, *"Dios me lleve al Peru"* (May God take me to Peru).

One reason for Puerto Rico's limited success with sugarcane in the sixteenth century was the island's vulnerability to attack and the accompanying hazards to shipping. Even after the Spanish colonization, the island continued to be a favorite target of the Carib Indians. One of the earliest places of refuge for the Tainos, the Spanish colonists, and the African slaves was the Dominican Convent, which was built on the headland of Old San Juan between 1523 and 1529. The first fort authorized by the Spanish crown was constructed between 1533 and 1540. Originally a walled patio with a circular tower overlooking San Juan Bay, the new *fortaleza* proved inadequate for defending the exposed headland and was later expanded to become the official governor's mansion, the handsome La Fortaleza that still serves the same purpose today.

In 1539, defense works were begun at the very tip of the headland. Fifty years later the great prow-shaped fortress of El Morro had taken form. But even then the protective edifice, constructed of huge stones brought as ballast in ships from Spain, required additional reinforcement. In the 1630's, a massive, encompassing city wall was undertaken. By the late 1700's, El Morro looked as it does today: a stalwart, multileveled battlement, laced with tunnels, and rising 140 feet above the sea.

The patio of Old San Juan's Dominican Convent, the monastery so named because it often served as a place of refuge for women and children

During the early 1500's competition was keen among the European powers for the prize islands of the West Indies, and Spain's holdings were frequently challenged. The French raided the southwestern town of San Germán as early as 1514 and repeated that action intermittently until the 1570's. By that time, Puerto Rico was known to have little wealth of its own. It had, however, become a strategic point on the route traveled by the Spanish treasure ships, laden with Peruvian gold and Mexican silver. Before heading across the Atlantic for the ports of Seville and Cádiz, the ships called at the harbor of San Juan, which was their final stopping place for taking on water and other supplies.

The sluggish economy of Puerto Rico could not possibly pay for the heavy fortifications, military garrison, and array of government

41

Views of the great prow-shaped battlement of El Morro

A *garita*, or sentry box, in the city wall,
which was constructed in the 1630's

officials necessary to protect the movement of Spain's imports from
its colonies, so the mother country ordered that funds should be
taken from the treasury of Mexico to subsidize the island's expendi-
tures. This annual contribution was known as the *situado*.

The monies were well spent, for El Morro successfully repulsed
the attack of the English admiral, Sir Francis Drake, in 1595. In
1598, Sir George Clifford, the Earl of Cumberland, tried again for a
British takeover, landing swiftly on the then-undefended beach east
of El Morro. Although his forces occupied San Juan for several
months, they were overcome by fever and dysentery and forced to
abandon their toehold on the island. Again, in 1925, a Dutch attack
resulted in a brief occupation and a burning of the city but ended
in a Spanish victory. Soon after these two nearly successful invasions
construction was begun on the city wall.

The seventeenth and eighteenth centuries brought long periods
of relative calm, even stagnation, for Puerto Rico. The defeat of the

Spanish Armada, sent to conquer England in 1588, had been costly and had started Spain on a long, slow period of decline. At the same time, the supplies of precious metals from the prosperous colonies of Mexico and of South America were beginning to be exhausted. Puerto Rico was left to its own devices and, despite a strict prohibition against trading with countries other than Spain, developed a lively illegal commerce. The island's main exports were now ginger, tobacco, and cattle hides. They were smuggled out to merchantmen that flew the flags of England, France, Denmark, and Holland. All of these European nations had acquired island possessions in the Caribbean, and there was an active exchange of tropically grown products for slaves, rum, and manufactured goods. Coffee growing was begun in Puerto Rico during the first half of the eighteenth century. It had first been introduced to nearby colonies, such as Haiti, by the French.

Puerto Rico's contraband trade, of course, brought no tax revenues into its treasury, and in 1765 Spain sent Field Marshal Alejandro O'Reilly, an Irish officer who had chosen service with the Spanish Army, to look into matters in the long-neglected colony. San Juan had developed as the island's social and economic center. The city had many churches and thick-walled houses with enclosed gardens. But public buildings and services suffered from the lack of funds. Even the *alcaldia* was uncompleted until near the end of the century.

O'Reilly found that the Spanish governor who had been appointed by the crown was a poor administrator, indifferent and pleasure loving. Laws were not enforced and corruption was widespread. A census conducted by the field marshal revealed the population of the island to be just under 45,000—only slightly larger than it had been in the Taino period 250 years earlier. About 5,000 of this number were black slaves; there was also a smaller free black population, and there were many mulattos among the 40,000 nonslave inhabitants.

Among O'Reilly's chief recommendations were military reforms, including the strengthening of San Juan's defenses. Accordingly, the Fort of San Cristóbal was built between 1766 and 1782 to flank El Morro near the eastern edge of the city wall. Its timely completion helped save Puerto Rico from the British for the third time when, in 1797, it was attacked by Sir Ralph Abercromby, who had just taken Spain's island of Trinidad for England.

Another of Field Marshal O'Reilly's suggestions was that the nearly dormant sugar industry should be revived. This measure, too, proved opportune, for with the outbreak of the American Revolution in 1775 the sugar exports of the British-held islands of Jamaica and Barbados were denied to the Thirteen Colonies. Spain granted Puerto Rico special permission to sell its sugar to the North Americans. Shortly after the Americans won their independence, the English king, probably anxious to reinforce his authority in the Caribbean, actually offered to give Gibraltar (which the British had captured in 1704) back to Spain if it would cede Puerto Rico to Great Britain. The Spanish considered the trade but refused it. Had Puerto Rico become a British possession in 1800, its destiny would no doubt have been very different.

The nineteenth century saw the beginnings of Puerto Rico's struggle for self-government. In 1808, Spain's power was weakened by the invasion of Napoleon, who deposed the king and placed his brother, Joseph Bonaparte, on the Spanish throne. Fired by the success of the American Revolution, independence movements had begun to gather force in Mexico and South America. And, in the Greater Antilles, which Spain had once claimed entirely, part of Hispaniola—Haiti—had already passed through French hands into independence. Santo Domingo, too, was reaching toward independence, while Jamaica had been ceded to England in 1670.

Only Cuba and Puerto Rico were still fully under Spanish control. To retain Puerto Rico's loyalty, the Spanish government-in-exile, which was headquartered in Cádiz, decreed that the island was no longer to be considered a colony but rather an overseas province of Spain, with full voting rights in the Cortes, the Spanish legislature.

Ramón Power y Giralt, a brilliant young Puerto Rican born of Spanish parents, went to Spain in 1810 to help draft the Constitution of 1812 and to win tax reforms and trading concessions for the hopeful islanders. But, by 1813, the thirty-eight-year-old Ramón Power was dead, stricken with yellow fever, and the withdrawal of Napoleon

45

had brought the Spanish king back to the throne and absolute monarchy back to Spain. The Constitution of 1812 was scrapped, and the Puerto Ricans were stripped of their newly won rights of citizenship.

In the decades that followed, the Spanish monarchy swung back and forth between absolutism and liberalism. From time to time the reigning king bent to constitutionalist pressures. But, on the whole, the Spanish governors that were appointed to Puerto Rico after 1820 were repressive and severe, for slave rebellions and revolutions of independence were now taking place in many parts of Latin America.

In Puerto Rico, however, conditions remained relatively stable as the island received an influx of Spanish colonials, still loyal to the mother country, from the newly independent nations of the West Indies and South America. Some years earlier, French colonial refugees had arrived from Haiti, and French and Spanish Louisianians had fled to Puerto Rico when that territory was purchased by the United States in 1803. The island, because of its considerable number of free blacks, had also long been a destination for runaway slaves. By 1840, its population had swelled to over 350,000. Slaves made up only about 10 percent of the total, while blacks and mulattos amounted to more than one-third of the free population.

If there appeared to be a lack of revolutionary fervor, a docility, perhaps even an apathy, among Puerto Ricans, several factors were responsible: those upper-class refugees from societies that had undergone revolutions formed an influential, conservative element in the population; the color barrier was not as marked or restrictive as on many other islands of the Caribbean; the slaves held in Puerto Rico were relatively few in number; and the small size of the island made revolutionary plots and guerrilla activity rather difficult to carry out.

Nonetheless, there were political thinkers, writers, and educators who felt strongly about the indignity of Puerto Rico's position as a colonial possession of Spain. In the latter half of the nineteenth century, free speech, freedom of the press, and the right of assembly were still denied under Spanish law, and slavery still existed.

A leading advocate of independence for Puerto Rico was Dr. Ramón Emeterio Betances, a physician and political activist who had

El Grito de Lares, a painting by Augusto Marín
in the Museum of Puerto Rican Art

long dreamed of a federation of Greater Antillean independent
states. Although he was forced to leave Puerto Rico because of his
revolutionary ideas, he continued his work in Santo Domingo and
in New York and directed from afar the uprising known as the Grito
de Lares, or Cry of Lares.

On the night of September 23, 1868, a group of several hundred
men and women involved in the movement for a free Puerto Rico
met at a farm near the mountain town of Lares. The following day
they advanced into the town and proclaimed the birth of the Republic of Puerto Rico.

The short-lived revolution was, however, a failure. The arms
shipped to the conspirators by Betances had been discovered en route
and had never arrived. The revolutionists were poorly prepared and
had little public support, for the majority of the island's liberals pre-
ferred change by evolutionary means. Some of the leaders of the

47

Lares uprising were killed by government troops, while others were jailed. Although sporadic skirmishes took place for some time afterward, no similar act of defiance against Spain was repeated.

The Grito de Lares has remained a solitary symbol of Puerto Rican resistance, and a white obelisk was erected in the plaza of Lares inscribed with the names of the heroes of that event. But violent revolutionary activity is so little feared on the island that, in 1969, the governor decreed September 24 an official holiday to commemorate annually the Cry of Lares.

In seeking the abolition of slavery, the leaders who favored autonomy for Puerto Rico were more successful. In addition to Ramón Emeterio Betances, they included Eugenio María de Hostos and Román Baldorioty de Castro. The latter was imprisoned because of his demands for self-government and later exiled by the Spanish authorities. Yet on March 22, 1873, (the same year that Spain became a republic for the brief period of two years) slavery was abolished in Puerto Rico. Of a population of 600,000, there were only about 30,000 slaves, for their number had been shrinking slowly as some bought their freedom and others were released from bondage by their masters. But at last the abhorrent institution was officially prohibited.

Autonomy, if not outright independence, was the next hurdle, and the year 1882 saw the formation of the Autonomist Party in Puerto Rico. An alliance with one of the political parties of Spain seemed the best way of peacefully achieving a measure of home rule for the island. And so the autonomist leader, Luis Muñoz Rivera, who had been born in the Puerto Rican mountain town of Barranquitas, went to Spain in 1897 and made a pact with the leader of the monarchy's Liberal Party, Mateo Práxedes Sagasta. The latter agreed that if his party came to power that year he would put forth a Charter of Autonomy for Puerto Rico.

One reason for Spain's willingness to look with favor on a home-rule charter for Puerto Rico was the violent agitation for independence that had been taking place in Cuba and which had erupted into a revolution in 1895. Puerto Rico, too, had its *independentistas*, and Spain deemed it wiser to satisfy the demands of Puerto Rico's non-

Sculptured head of the autonomist Román Baldorioty de Castro,
in the Ateneo Puertorriqueño

revolutionary liberals. In any case, the Spanish Liberal Party did come to power in 1897, and the promised charter based on the Sagasta Pact was granted.

Now Puerto Rico was to have its own two-house legislature, one elected and the other with an elected majority and an appointed minority. All males over twenty-five could vote, and the island was free to make its own trade agreements and, to an extent, control its own economy. However, as Puerto Rico was to be, in effect, a dominion, its governor would continue to be appointed by Spain. But his powers would be more limited than heretofore.

49

Surely the most stunning feature of the Charter of Autonomy of 1897 was the right of Puerto Rico to have voting representatives in the two houses of the Spanish Cortes, the body that made the laws that would affect any further changes in the island's status. Today, as a commonwealth of the United States, Puerto Rico does not have voting representatives in the United States Congress.

It will never be known whether the Charter of 1897 would have worked out as well in practice as it promised on paper, for the very next year a drastic change took place. The Spanish-American War broke out, and Puerto Rico—as one of the spoils along with the Philippines and Guam—was handed over by Spain to the victorious United States.

The immediate provocation for the war was the blowing up of the battleship *Maine* in Havana harbor on February 15, 1898, presumably under orders from Spain. But an underlying cause was the nineteenth-century expansionism of the United States. Having reached its continental limits of development, the nation was now looking toward the Caribbean with thoughts of turning it into an "American lake."

For some time the United States Government and large American corporations had supported Cuba's independence from Spain as a means of extending American sugar interests on that island. The disaster in Havana harbor was quickly parlayed into the battle cry, "Remember the Maine!" and public fury against Spain was fanned by the press lords, Hearst and Pulitzer, whose newspapers favored big business.

In April of 1898, President McKinley declared that a state of war existed with Spain, and in May, United States ships briefly bombarded El Morro, which represented another unwelcome symbol of Spain's presence in the Caribbean. On July 25, 1898, an American force of 16,000 landed in horseshoe-shaped Guánica Bay on the south coast of Puerto Rico and overcame the Spanish standing army of 8,000 in a series of skirmishes that lasted about two weeks. The population stood by dazed and, for the most part, welcoming.

While political independence for Cuba was a cause and a pre-

A statue in Ponce's Plaza Degetau of leader of autonomy movement
Luis Muñoz Rivera, who died in 1916

dictable result of the Spanish-American War, there was never any
intention of liberation for Puerto Rico. Even before the landing at
Guánica, the United States Government and press were making it
known that Puerto Rico was considered unready for self-government
and that the island would be taken over, partly as compensation for

war expenses and also because it would make an excellent naval base. In a proclamation of July 28, 1898, the American commander, Major General Nelson A. Miles, assured the Puerto Rican people that his occupation troops had come "in the cause of liberty, justice, and humanity . . . to promote your prosperity, and to bestow upon you the immunities and blessings of the liberal institutions of our Government."

Although Spain relinquished the island peacefully and the Puerto Ricans showed no hostility to the takeover, a military government was installed and lasted two years. The pleas of Luis Muñoz Rivera and Eugenio María de Hostos for an early end to the military regime went unheeded. As for autonomy, partial or complete, one of the military governors, Brigadier General George W. Davis, asserted, "Puerto Rico, unlike Dominica, Haiti, and Venezuela and many other republics, never was, is not and probably never will be independent."

The military governors from 1898 to 1900 initiated a program for the "Americanization" of Puerto Rico. The official policy was to implant United States' institutions, influencing education, culture, and the economy. It also was designed to instill Puerto Ricans with patriotism for the United States along with American values, goals, and ideals. For the convenience of Americans, the island's name was "simplified" to Porto Rico. The word *porto* does not exist in either Spanish or English.

When the transfer from a military to a civil government did take place, it was with the assurance, in the words of the United States consul, that "In the providence of God she [Puerto Rico] is ours today; she will be ours forever." The Congressional measure known as the Foraker Act (or the first Organic Act) established the form of civil government that commenced in 1900. The act provided for a governor, nonmilitary, but with broad powers, to be appointed by the president of the United States. The island would have a local legislature, the lower house popularly elected but the upper house also appointed by the president. To vote for members of the lower house, Puerto Ricans had to be male and had to meet literacy and property-owning requirements. As about 85 percent of the island's one million inhabitants were illiterate, the overwhelming majority had no vote. Practically, this hardly seemed to matter, for the United States Congress could override any legislation passed on the local level. As for Puerto Rican representation in Congress, there was an elected "United States Resident Commissioner" who could speak in the House of Representatives but who could not vote.

With no vote in Congress—which had full control of the island's destiny—no constitution, no citizenship, and no effective suffrage, the island was truly a colony. It *was* exempt from the payment of taxes to the United States Government. In this single respect, the United States seemed to recall its own colonial struggle with England when it had urgently put forth the protest, "No taxation without representation!"

One of the strongest tools of Americanization in the early decades of the century was the teaching of English as the primary language in the public schools of Puerto Rico. This practice followed the reasoning of one of the presidential-appointed commissioners of education who argued that, as long as there were so many illiterates to educate, why teach them Spanish when they might just as well learn English? Although this unrealistic approach never worked, teachers were imported for a period from the United States. At the same time, schools were built and named after American heroes and presidents; the American flag was saluted, and patriotic songs and hymns were sung in English. American national holidays—Washington's Birthday, Memorial Day, Flag Day—were observed and celebrated with appropriate displays of loyalty. But Puerto Rican holidays like Discovery Day and Three Kings Day, which were part of the island's 400-year-old history and culture, were glossed over; in fact, teachers were forced to work on Three Kings Day, which was the Puerto Rican Christmas.

When Luis Muñoz Rivera, who served as United States Resident Commissioner from 1911 to 1916, pointed out that Puerto Ricans were being denied "American liberties under the American flag," he was labeled a "malcontent" by the island's governor. On the economic scene, American sugar industrialists took over the cane fields, expanding them into large plantations at the expense of island farmers with small holdings who had formerly grown a diversity of crops.

In 1917, just before the United States entered World War I, Puerto Ricans received American citizenship. This new status was conferred through the Jones Act (or second Organic act). The responsibilities of citizenship included being liable for the military draft. Subsequently, 18,000 Puerto Ricans served in the war as members of the United States armed forces, which were at that time racially segregated. Many were sent to the Panama Canal to guard it against attack.

Muñoz Rivera, prior to his death in 1916, had asked that before the Jones Bill was passed into law a plebiscite be held to determine whether the islanders wanted United States citizenship. This vote was never taken and the new status was, in effect, imposed rather than offered. Those Puerto Ricans who refused American citizenship— about 300 people—were penalized by being stripped of their right to vote and to hold public office in Puerto Rico. They became pariahs among their own people and aliens on the island of their birth.

Among its other features, the Jones Act extended the vote to all Puerto Rican males over twenty-one regardless of literacy or property holdings, and it transformed the upper house of the island legislature into an elected body. But the power to veto local legislation still rested with Washington. Even though Puerto Ricans were now citizens, they still could not vote in United States' elections and had no voting representation in Congress. Thus there was no way in which they could express their opposition to any future wars in which they would be required to serve. Nor had they been granted any channel of expression regarding the island's future status.

In 1922, the island's independence advocates formed the Nationalist Party. They charged that the United States had illegally stripped Puerto Rico of its autonomous status in 1898 and, therefore, was obliged to restore the rights it had then enjoyed. As the decade drew to a close, conditions worsened, and the Nationalists drew increased support. Four giant United States sugar corporations now owned nearly half of Puerto Rico's cane fields. Despite the law limiting farms to 500 acres, the absentee-owned cane lands averaged 40,000 acres each. Work in the cane fields not only paid poorly but was seasonal, leaving the workers unemployed six months of the year.

Under the old Spanish *patrón* system, farmworkers had been allowed some land of their own on which to grow vegetables and raise livestock. But they could do so no longer. Now foodstuffs and other necessities—cornmeal, lard, beans, dairy items, meats, shoes, and clothing—began to be imported from the United States. As they had to be shipped long distances and were subject to a tariff, they cost far more than when they had been produced by home industries. Impoverished country people began to move to San Juan in search of work, living in squatters' huts in urban slums. Disease and demoralization were rampant.

Suffering intensified during the depression years of the 1930's. Colonel Theodore Roosevelt, the island's governor from 1929 to 1932, reported openly on conditions and blamed his government's policies. He was the son of President Theodore Roosevelt, who in his Rough Rider days had called the Spanish-American conflict a "splendid little war." He had also lamented, however, that, "It wasn't much of a war but it was all the war there was."

In 1932, when Franklin Delano Roosevelt became president, the island's problems began to receive some official recognition. In that year, too, the use of the name Puerto Rico, properly spelled, was officially reinstated. In forthright language, Harold L. Ickes, the Secretary of the Interior, declared that unfettered capitalism had reduced the island to "virtual economic serfdom." And he summed up, "There is today more widespread misery and destitution and far more unemployment in Puerto Rico than at any previous time in its history."

The decade of the 1930's also saw the emergence of a dramatic figure, Pedro Albizu Campos, as leader of the island's Nationalist Party. Albizu Campos was a mulatto of medium-dark skin color. He had taken a law degree at Harvard and served as an officer in World War I. His experiences in the United States and particularly in the segregated armed forces had provided him with a broad exposure to American racism and had fanned his militancy as an *independentista*.

The Nationalist movement erupted into violence in 1936 when two young men killed the island's police chief, E. Francis Riggs. After being taken into custody the youths were shot to death in the police station on the unproven charge that they were trying to escape. Subsequently, Albizu Campos and seven followers were arrested, charged with conspiracy to overthrow the United States Government in Puerto Rico, and jailed in Federal prison in Atlanta, Georgia.

The year after the shooting an even more violent disturbance took place. On March 21, 1937, a group of Nationalists planned a march and rally in Ponce and secured the required permit. The day was Palm Sunday. At the last moment, permission for the program was revoked by the island's governor, Blanton Winship, a retired army general. The Nationalists decided to hold the march as planned and, as the parade peacefully proceeded up a Ponce street to the strains of "La Borinqueña," the police opened fire. Twenty people died, eighteen of them marchers, and over one hundred were wounded, mostly bystanders. The Palm Sunday tragedy has since been known as the Massacre of Ponce.

A strong sentiment for independence also marked the early years of Luis Muñoz Marín, son of Luis Muñoz Rivera. Muñoz Marín was born in 1898, the year of the American takeover of Puerto Rico. He was destined to be the island's key figure of the mid-twentieth century and, as he has often been called, "the architect of modern Puerto Rico."

In his adolescent years, Muñoz Marín spent time in Washington, D.C., where his father was Resident Commissioner. As a young man in the 1920's, he lived in New York City's Greenwich Village and was at the center of a flourishing literary and artistic scene. As a poet, translator, and writer, he promoted Puerto Rican culture. Even more importantly, his critical pieces published in thoughtful periodicals and newspapers called attention to conditions in Puerto Rico.

In the 1930's, considered too radical for Puerto Rico's Liberal Party of which he had been a member, he was expelled and with other advocates of self-government formed the Partido Popular Democrático (Popular Democratic Party) in 1938. The PDP, or Popu-

The *jíbaro* in his *pava,* immortalized in the painting *El Pan Nuestro*
by Ramón Frade; from the Museum of Puerto Rican Art

lares as they soon became known, took up the *jíbaro,* the peasant of
Puerto Rico's mountainous interior, as their representative figure.
The *jíbaro* image embodied patience, hard work, dignity, and an
intuitive intelligence—traditional Puerto Rican virtues. The *pava,*

the wide-brimmed straw hat of the *jíbaro,* became the PDP symbol, instantly recognizable to those voters who could not read. The party's slogan was *Pan, Tierra y Libertad* (Bread, Land, and Liberty).

The word *independence* was noticeably absent, for Muñoz Marín felt that a host of other problems needed to be addressed first. They included the enforcement of the 500-acre law to help redistribute the sugar lands to the landless farmers, a farm-credit system, the promotion of local industry, slum clearance, changes in the educational system, and numerous social reforms. His campaign of 1940 was carried out largely in the rural interior as an exhausting personal odyssey. His aim was to secure PDP support from those farmers who, in the past, had sold their votes to the prosugar interests for a bribe of a couple of dollars or a pair of new shoes.

In the election of 1940, the PDP squeaked through to a slim majority with 37 percent of the votes, winning just enough seats in the Puerto Rican Senate so that Muñoz Marín could be named president of that legislative body. This political post was the most important one on the island that a Puerto Rican could occupy at that time.

The next ten years brought both wartime hardships and political progress. Although the depression ended with United States' involvement in World War II (1941-1945), Nazi submarines in the Caribbean endangered the supply lines to the United States air and naval installations on Puerto Rico. No longer self-sufficient in foodstuffs, islanders suffered skyrocketing prices and often hunger, for the requirements of the military came first. Over 65,000 Puerto Ricans served, mainly abroad, in World War II. And 43,000 saw service in the ensuing Korean War.

On the political front, several of Muñoz Marín's programs began to be implemented under the sympathetic and effective governorship of Rexford Guy Tugwell, who had been appointed by President Franklin Roosevelt in 1941. Tugwell, who vividly recorded conditions in "the stricken land" in his book of the same name, took the sugar interests' violation of the 500-acre law into the courts, started electrification projects, established some local industry, and undertook wage and labor legislation.

On Tugwell's resignation in 1946, President Harry Truman appointed the first Puerto Rican, former Resident Commissioner Jesús T. Piñero, to the post of governor. He was the last to be appointed by the president, for in 1947 the Jones Act was amended, giving Puerto Ricans the right to elect their own governor. In the election of 1944, Luis Muñoz Marín, as leader of the PDP, had made a strong showing, and in 1948 he was elected governor. He took the oath of office and began his first term on January 2, 1949.

Along with an elected governor for the first time in its history, there soon came a change in the island's political status. World opinion in the postwar period was highly critical of colonialism, and the United States had to seek a new format for its relationship with the island. Luis Muñoz Marín, having abandoned the idea of independence because it appeared to him economically unfeasible, agreed to an Estado Libre Asociado or "free associated state." For lack of a more convenient English equivalent, the island in its new status was officially designated the Commonwealth of Puerto Rico.

On July 25, 1952, exactly fifty-four years after the United States takeover, Puerto Rico's Commonwealth Constitution went into effect. This document had been granted under Public Law 600, which was signed by President Truman in 1950 and had been accepted by Puerto Rican voters in 1951. As in 1917, when citizenship was conferred, the islanders were not asked to choose but simply to approve. The only alternative to approval of the new commonwealth status and its constitution was a continuation of the former status. There was no opportunity for an expression of choice among such options as commonwealth, statehood, or independence.

Under its Commonwealth Constitution, Puerto Rico was given the right to administer many of its internal affairs and was to be entitled to substantial Federal aid for highways, housing, health, education, and other public programs. Puerto Ricans became eligible for social security, unemployment insurance, and many other Federally funded social-welfare projects. The Puerto Rican flag, with its five broad horizontal stripes of red and white and its white star on a blue triangle, was for the first time permitted to be flown alongside

La Fortaleza, the governor's mansion, which has flown both the United States and Puerto Rican flags since 1952

the United States flag. The flag had been designed by Puerto Rican patriots in 1895.

The island, however, still did not control all of its affairs. In operations such as military protection, immigration, customs, foreign relations, foreign commerce and shipping, airports and airspace, currency and the postal system, radio and television licensing, the United States Federal Government retained full control. Thus, in many respects, Puerto Rico now appeared to resemble a state of the Union.

However, unlike the citizens of the forty-eight states that existed in 1952, Puerto Ricans still could not vote in presidential or other national elections and had no voting representatives in Congress. Accordingly, they still paid no Federal income taxes. Thus the "free associated state" was certainly not a state in the sense that New York, Ohio, or California were states. On the other hand, Puerto Rico was not a sovereign body, for its association with the United States was a binding one and its freedom to break that association was completely in the hands of a Congress in which it had no voting power.

While most Puerto Ricans saw commonwealth as a practical step, those who favored independence—then the second strongest political coalition on the island—denounced it as glorified colonialism. They charged that the new status was motivated in part by the United States' discomfort at having to report to the United Nations on its "non-self-governing territory."

At the same time, the stabilization of the island's status opened it to United States business investment on an unprecedented scale. Under the attractive terms of an economic development plan known as Operation Bootstrap, mainland businesses were offered both Federal and island tax exemption, as well as a labor force that would work for wages far below those of the mainland.

Spurred by *independentista* sentiment on the island, terrorist outbursts took place in Washington, D.C., the first in 1950, shortly after President Truman had signed Public Law 600. Two Puerto Rican Nationalists fired on Blair House guards in what was believed to be an attempt on the president's life. As the White House was being renovated at the time, the president was then living in this smaller nearby residence. In 1954, four Puerto Rican residents of New York City opened fire in the United States House of Representatives, wounding five Congressmen.

61

In Puerto Rico, however, majority support for the Commonwealth and for its advocate and authority figure, Luis Muñoz Marín, continued. Reelected in 1952, 1956, and 1960, Muñoz Marín served a total of four terms as governor. In 1964, preferring to have the PDP develop other leaders, he chose not to run and backed Roberto Sánchez Vilella. Although lacking the personal appeal and political acumen of the older man, Sánchez Vilella did win the governorship that year.

During his term, in 1967, a long-desired plebiscite on the political status of Puerto Rico was finally held. Although the United States made it clear in advance that the plebiscite was merely an opinion poll and would in no way bind it to action, Puerto Rican voters were asked to record their preference for either commonwealth, statehood, or independence.

Muñoz Marín campaigned vigorously for votes to sustain the Commonwealth, while most *independentistas* boycotted the plebiscite on the ground that participation in it was a mockery because it was not binding. The outcome showed 60.41 percent for commonwealth, 38.98 percent for statehood, and .06 percent for independence. However, only 65.9 percent of the registered voters had participated in the plebiscite; 34.1 percent had abstained.

Although the Populares seemed securely in control, the 1968 gubernatorial election brought a surprise, caused by a split in the PDP ranks, and in a three-way contest Luis A. Ferré, the candidate of the prostatehood New Progressive Party, formed in 1967, came to office. Ferré, born in 1904, was an industrialist and art philanthropist from Ponce, who had previously been affiliated with the island's prostatehood Republican Party, which dated from 1900. His administration reinforced the building of the new Puerto Rico with its emphasis on industrialization and the Americanization of the economy. Although, as a candidate, Ferré had declared that status was not an issue in the election, he saw statehood as a not-far-distant goal and attempted to press for it while in office.

The elections of 1972 and 1976 brought two more political reversals, which seemed to be mainly responses to the island's economic disappointments and growing social problems. Ferré was defeated in 1972 and succeeded by the PDP candidate, Rafael Hernández Colón. Four years later, in 1976, the PDP once more gave way to the NPP as the prostatehood candidate, Carlos Romero Barceló, came to office.

Thus the long gubernatorial tenure of Luis Muñoz Marín—from 1949 to 1964—has been followed by shifting electoral choices, both of the man and the party, strongly suggesting that the question of the island's status is still far from being resolved.

Yet, whatever problems it may have caused, the commonwealth period, inaugurated in 1952, has molded Puerto Rican life into what it is today, economically, socially, and politically. And certainly the influence of the Americanization policy on the Indian-Spanish-African roots of the Puerto Rican people has created a broad cultural blend that is unique in today's Caribbean world.

·III·
A Caribbean People Today

More than any other people in the Americas, Puerto Ricans can be said to be living "between two worlds." No islander, even in the remote mountainous interior, is untouched by influences that can clearly be traced to the United States. Examples of this phenomenon are everywhere. In a poor and isolated board shack, high in the Maricao State Forest, a washing machine whirs and the small children of the family sit watching a morning program on color television. Rural electrification and an extended-credit purchase plan, accomplishments of American technology and finance, are responsible.

In San Juan, the two cultures meet at every turn. Most signs are in Spanish, but the products advertised have United States' brand names. During rush hours, heavy traffic clogs the roads as Puerto Ricans commute between their city jobs and the "bedroom" suburbs in which they live. The cars in which they inch their way through the *tapón*, or "bottle stopper" traffic jams, are mostly American-manufactured. And the dwellings of their *urbanizaciones*, or single-family tract-house developments, have been built to meet the standards of the Federal Housing Administration so that they can qualify for construction and mortgage loans from American banks.

Cockfights compete with baseball for the spectator-sports fan's dollar. A jukebox blares rock music at one restaurant while a Puerto Rican string trio serenades diners at another. In 1978, San Juan holds its first Saint Patrick's Day Parade, and a small but enthusiastic crowd of fifty attends. In the coffee shop of a large department store in the enormous Las Americas shopping mall, one can have a tuna-fish sandwich for lunch or an elaborately constructed meat-and-

Children of a mountain community in the Río Abajo State Forest,
who may bear a trace of Taino ancestry

plantain pie that is a tradition of Puerto Rican cuisine. No wonder
the writer René Marqués describes his fellow islanders as a "schizo-
phrenic society" with "two languages, two citizenships, two basic
philosophies of life. . . ."

The culture upon which the United States way of life was super-
imposed was a remarkably comfortable blend of Spanish and African
elements. Underlying these two was the Indian culture that had
been all but obliterated and is today the most difficult to trace.

The *jíbaro*, himself a vanishing species, was thought to carry the
strongest strains of Indian ancestry, for many of the Tainos fled to
the mountains in the early Spanish days. The very name *jíbaro* comes
from Jívaro, a tribe of fierce Amazonian Indians who hid themselves
away from the white man. But the heritage of the Puerto Rican
jíbaro was mixed, for runaway slaves, Spanish outlaws, and those

seeking simply to forsake island society also took refuge in the mountains in the course of centuries.

Nonetheless, the *jíbaro* way of life did seem most closely related to that of the Taino Indians. These Puerto Rican peasant-farmers lived in thatched-roof huts, which they called *bohíos*, they used handwoven hammocks for sleeping, and they were skilled at the weaving of fibers for baskets and other household articles. The folk Catholicism they practiced was in many ways similar to the religion of the Indians with its mystical rituals and herbal cures. And the *jíbaros* developed the art of carving and painting miniature hard-wood figures of the saints, called *santos*, which may have been derived from the *cemis*, or household gods, of the Tainos.

The twentieth century saw the destruction of the *jíbaro* culture. First came the single-crop sugar economy, then the electrification projects that flooded numerous acres of mountain farmland, and then the intense rural poverty and growing industrialization that drew country people to urban centers. A couple of decades ago the *jíbaro* was the hayseed, or country bumpkin, newly come to the city. Today, at the point of extinction, the *jíbaro* has gained the status of a Puerto Rican folk hero. He is recognized as having been a rural independent, proud and self-sufficient, as were his Indian forebears.

The Spanish conquest of the island brought it a highly developed culture, many elements of which were destined to long outlast Spain's 400-year occupation. Among the earliest influences were those of language, law, and, of course, architecture. Most of the towns built in Spain's New World colonies conformed to a design based on a central square, or plaza. Accordingly, the surrounding blocks were laid out in a grid, or checkerboard pattern. The plaza, not unlike the Indian *batey*, was used for military drill and also served as a public meeting ground and as a marketplace.

Today's walled city of Old San Juan is a living museum that offers a remarkably faithful picture of a Spanish colonial settlement. Its official founding date is 1521, preceding the Pilgrims' landing at Plymouth by a century. Only about seven blocks square, Old San Juan has several plazas, for the city expanded bit by bit. The plazas

Old figurines of *santos*, eight to nine inches high, on display
in the Santos Museum in Old San Juan

are now converted into quiet, restful parks. As the terrain inclined
sharply up to the promontory of El Morro, several streets were com-
posed of stone steps, and two of these narrow and picturesque "step
streets" remain today. Much of Old San Juan is paved with bluish-
gray stone blocks, or *adoquines*, which contain iron slag from Spanish foundries and were brought to Puerto Rico as ballast in Spanish
vessels.

67

In Old San Juan: a quiet, picturesque "step street"

By the first half of the twentieth century, the old city had begun to succumb to urban decay and to commercial-industrial inroads that threatened to destroy its unique character and its historical value. Fortunately, in 1949, the government declared Old San Juan

and the balconied facades of a busy shopping street

a historic zone in which no changes could be made without official approval. Through the Institute of Puerto Rican Culture, under the direction of Ricardo Alegría, a program of supervised restoration began. Owners of private houses received bank loans and tax exemptions for renovations that would preserve the softly colored facades, the wooden and wrought-iron balconies, tiled floors, and beamed ceilings of the old buildings.

Among the many small museums of Old San Juan is that of the Puerto Rican Family, housed on the second floor of a long, narrow building called La Casa del Callejón (The House on the Alley). While the building dates from the eighteenth century, the furnishings are those of the nineteenth century. Typical of those occupied by the prosperous small merchants of the city, the house shows a parlor, dining room, bedrooms, kitchen, and master's study, or office. All the rooms are laid out along a breezeway overlooking an inner court and have balconies facing onto the street. The merchant's stock in trade, varied wares and provisions mostly imported from Spain, were kept on the ground floor.

Just as in centuries past, today's Old San Juan has its bustling

The nineteenth-century parlor in the Museum of the Puerto Rican family

shopping neighborhoods. Its narrow streets are lined with small stores of every description that contrast sharply with the Sears, K-Marts, and Penneys of the sleek, new shopping centers on the outskirts of modern San Juan. Many Puerto Ricans who do not live in the old city prefer to come there to shop, claiming that it has the greatest variety of goods and the best bargains.

As Old San Juan also attracts many tourists from San Juan's beach-front hotels and is the site of the cruise-ship harbor, there are numerous art, jewelry, handicraft, and novelty stores. With its fortifications, churches, and other historical landmarks, its museums and galleries, its quiet streets and tree-shaded plazas, its restaurants and its unusual hotel, a transformed Carmelite convent, Old San Juan is a gemlike small city. It is also a community that is lived in and worked in, has a rich neighborhood life, and is as vibrant and functional today as it was in the peak years of the Spanish colonial period.

Another Spanish contribution to the island's development was agriculture. The new crops from Europe and the East not only expanded the economy but introduced an array of foods that helped to establish Puerto Rican cuisine as it exists today. Sugarcane was the earliest of the commercial plantings. By the 1520's, the first sugar mill, or *central*, was built, probably near Añasco on the west coast. There the cut cane was brought to be crushed. Indian workers and the first black slaves fed the stalks into the juice-extracting machinery, while oxen harnessed to hardwood poles supplied the power to drive the mechanism.

The very first foreign foods to be brought by the Spanish must have been bacalao (dried salt cod), dried chick peas, and rice. These staples of the Spanish diet kept well and were an important part of the ships' stores. Today the *bacalaito*, a deep-fried fritter of boiled shredded codfish, flour, water, garlic, and other seasonings, could almost be called the "hot dog of Puerto Rico." Tiny, crisp *bacalaitos fritos* are served as appetizers while larger, wafer-shaped codfish fritters make ample snacks. *Bacalao* can also be prepared in a stew with potatoes and other vegetables or in a *serenata*, a cold dish of flaked fish and raw onions dressed with oil and vinegar.

Garlic, onion, smoked pork products such as bacon, ham, and Spanish *chorizo* sausage were all flavorful enhancers unknown before they were introduced from Spain. The same was true of lard and other oils and fats used for flavoring and frying.

Chick peas, or *garbanzos*, joined the Indian-cultivated beans of the New World to become staples of the Puerto Rican diet. Today the roster of legumes eaten on the island includes red kidney beans, small pink, black, and white beans (*habichuelas coloradas, rosadas, negras,* and *blancas*), lima beans (*habas*), lentils (*lentejas*), and pigeon peas (*gandules*). Bean dishes are often prepared with a *sofrito*, a tasty sauce of the garlic, onion, salt pork, ham, and lard of the Old World married to the chili peppers and tomatoes of Mexico and introduced around the Caribbean in Spanish colonial days.

Rice is as typical an everyday food as beans, and the two are often eaten together, the beans in their *sofrito* spooned over the rice. Directly from Spain comes the popular *arroz con pollo* (rice with chicken), the rice colored deep yellow with *achiote* berries instead of saffron. A Puerto Rican rice dish is *asopao*, a soupy but hearty mixture of rice with some chicken or seafood in it. For an economy dish, an *asopao* can be made with pigeon peas. On the other hand, a holiday or special occasion calls for *lechón asado* (roast suckling pig), which is slowly cooked out of doors on a turnspit over a charcoal fire.

The cornmeal of the Tainos often turns up in today's Puerto Rico as *surullitos*, crisp, deep-fried corn sticks shaped like small cigars and served either as an appetizer or main-dish accompaniment. Country people prepare baked *surullitos*, as large as bananas, which they eat with coffee as an early-morning first breakfast before going out to the fields. But, due to moist growing conditions on most of the island, corn has never been as plentiful or widely used as the versatile plantain, which, along with the banana, traveled from the East Indies to the West Indies via Africa. European traders and slavers and African slaves were the first to transport these foods to the New World.

Unlike the sweet, ready-to-eat, yellow banana (*guineo*), the plantain (*plátano*), whether its skin is green or yellow, must be cooked

72

to be eaten. Boiled, mashed, baked, fried, or stuffed, it is the Puerto Rican counterpart of the Irish, or white, potato. *Plátanos* come to the table most often as *tostones*, crisp-fried slices of green plantain that are served the way French fries are in the United States, with just about everything. Some cooked dishes specifically call for the slightly sweeter, but still bland and starchy, *amarillo*. Although this yellow plantain is called "ripe," it still must be cooked to be eaten. And to make matters even more complicated, there are Puerto Rican recipes that require green bananas (*guineitos*) and those that insist on the thumb-size finger bananas known as *guineitos niños* ("green-banana children"). A Puerto Rican specialty that brings together plantains, garlic, and crisp pork cracklings (called *chicharrón*) is the dumplinglike *mofongo*, for which the cooked plantain is pounded, seasoned, and shaped into large balls—about two inches in diameter—that are served hot.

Bland, starchy tubers, introduced from Africa, are also basics of the Puerto Rican diet. Whether at the big, modern supermarket, the neighborhood *colmado* (grocery store), or the roadside stand, there is always an array of these large, variously shaped vegetables with their rough and even hairy brown exteriors. Among them are the *yautía* (tanier), the *ñame* (African yam), and the *batata* (a white or very pale yellow "sweet" potato). But the last two are not to be confused with the sweet, golden yam or sweet potato of the southern United States. Boiled, these African tubers resemble coarse-textured, unseasoned white potato. The native *yuca* (cassava) of the Tainos is regularly available, as are the chayote and the *calabaza* ("pumpkin"), two West Indian squashes. The pear-shaped chayote resembles a summer squash and is often stuffed with meat or cheese, while the firm, orange-fleshed *calabaza,* which is more like an acorn squash, is used in soups, stews, and fritters.

Once the breadfruits, dangling from their shiny-leaved trees, have ripened, these bumpy-skinned green globes are brought to market. Like the plaintain, the bland-tasting breadfruit cannot be eaten raw. This South Pacific mainstay that has become a Caribbean staple can also be used for making *tostones.*

For snacks and light meals, Puerto Ricans are exceptionally fond

Holding up a chayote (top) and a *batata* (bottom) at the farmers' market in the Río Piedras district of San Juan

of *pasteles* and *pastelillos*. Despite similar names, the two are very different. *Pasteles* are really distant cousins of Mexican tamales, for they are made with a paste, or masa, of mashed plantain and mashed *yautía*, instead of mashed corn. The paste is stuffed with a savory meat center that includes *garbanzos* and raisins, and it is then wrapped in a plantain leaf and cooked in water. Like the cornhusk that is wrapped around the Mexican *tamal*, or "bundle," the plantain leaf enclosing the *pastel* is not eaten. The *pastelillo*, on the other hand, is a fried pastry turnover, shaped like a half-moon and filled with a meat, crab, cheese, or other mixture. On some parts of the islands, the *pastelillo* is called an *empanadilla*, or "little pie."

In the sugar-rich Caribbean, desserts tend to be sweet, and there are several variations on the Spanish flan, or caramel custard, in which fresh coconut is used. *Tembleque* is a shivery white pudding that is made with cornstarch and coconut milk. The latter is not the watery liquid found in the cavity of the coconut but rather a "milk" squeezed from grated fresh coconut meat. The dessert called *Bien Me Sabe* consists of a creamy, egg-rich coconut sauce poured over sponge cake. *Bien Me Sabe* translates as "it tastes good to me." The use of coconut also extends to the island's most famous drink, the *piña colada*. So rich it is almost a dessert, the *piña colada* is prepared with a sweetened and thickened extract called cream of coconut, which is combined with pineapple juice, crushed ice, and Puerto Rican rum.

Tropical fruits like guava and papaya are candied in syrup. The egg-size guavas are usually preserved in halves called "shells," while the melonlike papayas are cut into strips. When served as dessert, they are usually combined with bland white cheese to counteract their sweetness. Fresh fruits include musky, delicate-fleshed papaya and juicy, field-ripened pineapple.

Island-grown coffee is dark, strong, and deep-flavored. It was once a favorite of the Vatican, to which it was regularly exported, but production is nowadays very limited. When it is served black after dinner in a small cup, or demitasse, it is called *café negro*.

In addition to their foods and dining customs, the Spanish introduced a social structure in which classes were stratified and a strict code of manners prevailed. As in all the Spanish colonies of the New World, the *peninsulares,* those Spanish subjects born on the Iberian Peninsula, held a higher rank in Puerto Rican society than did the *criollos,* or creoles, people of Spanish blood who were born on the island. Although the distinction between the two later died, both poor whites and nonwhites refer, even today, to people of privilege as *blanquitos,* "little whites."

The Spanish family pattern was highly paternalistic. The husband and master was not only *macho* (strong and dominant) but possessed a dignity that required the unflinching respect of his family and peers. To be accused of being *sin vergüenza* (without shame) was the most serious of slurs. The qualities of *machismo* (manliness) and *dignidad* (dignity) are still important values in Puerto Rican life today.

In early island society, the wife devoted herself exclusively to her family and her home, the daughters were well-chaperoned at all times, and the sons were sent to Spain for their schooling and early adventuring. Courtship was strictly supervised to protect the innocence of the unmarried young woman, and marriage was solemnly undertaken and regarded as permanent.

Not all of the islanders conformed to the rigid values of the Spanish ruling class. Most of the first colonists had arrived womanless and had formed liaisons with either Indian or, later, with African women, and there soon developed a mestizo population. As weddings were costly and required the approval of the church, many of the mixed unions were consensual, that is by mutual consent and not formalized by any civil or religious authority. In the face of this trend, the older Spanish families attempted to preserve their *sangre pura* (pure blood) through a strict selection of marriage partners.

Today most Puerto Ricans admit that, after centuries of island life, no such thing as *sangre pura* exists. Though many Puerto Ricans do have their racial preferences when it comes to marriage, most do not draw a sharp line on the issue of color. Family disagreements, if they do occur, are usually easily healed, for Puerto

76

A racially mixed bridal couple and members of their
wedding party at San Juan Cathedral

Ricans like many islanders have a strong sense of their cultural
isolation and uniqueness as a people. A young woman from a predominantly white family in Ponce told of a young male cousin who
had recently chosen a black wife. Despite earlier objections, in a
very short time the bride was taken into the bosom of the family,
"because she is one of us now and we love her." Similarly, in the
mestizo marriage that may produce children of various skin colors,
Puerto Ricans say that it is often the darkest-skinned child who is
the most loved.

Puerto Ricans appear to be highly conscious of skin color, for
they use a variety of descriptive words to differentiate among the
various gradations and tones. Terms include *trigueño* (tan, olive-
skinned), *prieto* (dark-complexioned), and *negro* (black). But this
color consciousness should not be confused with prejudice.

At the same time, there is a puzzling duality of feeling about the
desirability of certain racial characteristics. The word *negra* (black

woman), for example, is often used as a term of endearment, equivalent to "dear" or "darling," for a woman of any color. Kinky hair, on the other hand, is automatically described as *pelo malo*, bad hair.

In matters of employment, it has long been true that darker-skinned white-collar workers were much more likely to be found in public-administration jobs than in banks and other private businesses. This picture has been changing. In large part, it is a reflection of the civil rights movement in the United States during the 1960's, which resulted in the breaking of many racial barriers in American enterprises on the island.

The Puerto Rican experience of life in the United States is considerable because of the large migration to the mainland during the past few decades. The American tendency to categorize Puerto Ricans as either black or white has caused much misery and consternation. If anything, it has reinforced the intense pride of Puerto Ricans in their culture and in their view of their society as an ethnic-racial entity.

Perhaps the best way to sum up the Puerto Rican attitude on racial matters is to say that, while there is certainly an awareness of skin color on the island, darker skins are not the impediment to marriage and social standing or to economic and professional opportunity that they long have been in the United States.

Along with the traditions of family life, the Spanish introduced the Roman Catholic religion to Puerto Rico. The Dominican friars began the building of the Church of San José in 1532. As other communities grew up around the island, the church became their central feature, usually providing a school and a hospital as well. Many of the Indians and Africans were converted to Catholicism and the Spanish *patrones*, unlike the majority of Anglo-Saxon slave owners in the Americas, often brought their slaves to church services with them and encouraged them to marry in a religious ceremony.

The Spanish religion, however, was closely allied with the colonial government and was essentially an elite institution. The clergy was made up of *peninsulares*, and Puerto Ricans were not trained for the priesthood. In part, this policy was due to fear that island-born priests might become leaders of uprisings against Spain. Another reason for the exclusion of Puerto Ricans from religious leadership was the question of racial purity. Applicants with Indian or African blood could not be ordained.

Because the policies of the church were one with those of Spain, the church also opposed the abolition of slavery. And so, in a number of ways, it did not meet the needs of the island's varied and growing population. Gradually, therefore, a kind of folk religion developed. It combined elements of the old Taino beliefs and practices and of African tribal religion along with the most appealing aspects of Roman Catholicism.

While regular church attendance and confession tended to be ignored by the majority of the people, Catholic saints' days were and still are widely observed around the island. Each town has its patron saint and expresses its love of ceremony and celebration in its *fiesta patronal* lasting a week or slightly longer. About eighty such festivals take place during the year. Especially interesting, with its grotesque masks and colorful costumes, is that of *Santiago Apóstal*, Saint James the Apostle, which takes place in July at Loíza Aldea. This town and the nearby larger town of Loíza were places of settlement for local sugar-plantation slaves, who were freed in 1873, and so have large black populations whose ancestry can be traced to specific tribal groups in West Africa.

A religious ritual that may be related to the outdoor prayer gatherings of both the Tainos and of African groups is the *rogativa*, a meeting or procession for a specific purpose, such as to invoke rain. In Old San Juan's Plazuela de la Rogativa, there is a dramatic sculpture group that represents a bishop accompanied by marching women carrying torches. An inscription at the base of the statuary relates that according to legend this *rogativa*, with its women's prayers to Saint Ursula and the Eleven Thousand Virgins, brought about the liberation of the capital from the British in the siege of 1797.

The American takeover of Puerto Rico in 1898 separated the Catholic church from the government and saw the introduction of

A grotesque mask used in the *fiesta patronal* at Loíza Aldea,

those Protestant faiths that predominated on the mainland. Largely through missionary activity, conversions were made to the Baptist, Methodist, Presbyterian, and other denominations. Most popular, however, were the revivalist sects with their emotional appeal and evangelistic public gatherings. Today there are many small, home-grown revivalist offshoots that are housed in storefront churches

and a *rogativa* represented in sculpture in Old San Juan

both on the island and in the Puerto Rican barrios of North American cities.

Completely outside the realm of organized religion is *espiritismo*, or spiritism, a belief in the efficacy of magic potions, spells, incantations, and herbal remedies for illnesses, emotional difficulties, and a host of personal problems. Spiritism is practiced by lay consultants

A spiritist shop in the Río Piedras farmers' market

who have built up strong followings. Many such practitioners can be found in the black community of Loíza, and spiritist shops are stocked with a wide variety of preparations. Among them are herbs, both fresh and in dried mixtures, numerous kinds of candles, some in the shape of human figures, and gourds, rattles, and brooms for driving out evil spirits.

Thus, while 99 percent of Puerto Ricans are considered to be Christians—with about 80 percent Roman Catholic and the rest belonging to Protestant faiths—most appear to practice an unorthodox mixture of local customs and church rituals. Parents who live together in a consensual union, for example, may insist on taking their baby to church for baptism. Crucifixes, pictures of Jesus, and statuettes of the saints may well adorn the home of a family that never steps inside the portals of a church. On the other hand, a family that takes the sacraments, including last rites for its dying, may also adhere to the practice of keeping a bowl of fruit on the table for the nighttime visits of departed spirits, in the tradition of the vanished Tainos of Boriquén.

Language, like religion, is an aspect of Puerto Rican culture that has shown a stubborn resistance to Americanization. Between 1898 and the 1930's, efforts to make English the language of instruction in the elementary grades of the public schools failed to produce English-speaking Puerto Rican children. Learning, in fact, was so inhibited that over two-thirds of the population remained illiterate by 1940. Spanish is now the language of instruction in most public educational facilities (and has been since 1949), and English is taught as a second language from the earliest grades. Literacy in Spanish is now reported to be over 90 percent on the island. But proficiency in English remains low. As a dean of the University of Puerto Rico says of the English-language studies, "Our public-education program produces high-school graduates who have had twelve years of *not* learning English."

The imposition of the English language on the Spanish-speaking island in 1898 soon created a rift in Puerto Rican society. As English became the language of government, finance, and business, those families who supported the presence of the United States and had the most to gain from it began to send their children to private schools where English was well taught, and from those island institutions to universities in the United States. Today in Puerto Rico, it is still true that an English-language education, in connection with a full roster of Spanish studies, is an avenue of opportunity. Although private-school fees are high, many less prosperous families struggle to give their children this dual advantage.

For those Puerto Ricans attending public schools, where English is generally poorly taught, some facility in that language is most often gained through a job or through other outside contacts. Young people tend to speak a "youth culture" English, picked up in part from the words of popular songs. "Spanglish" is the name given to a hybrid Spanish that is infused with words of English origin like *el coat, el hamburger, los tineyers* (teen-agers), *los jipis* (hippies).

In any case, most Puerto Ricans acquire only a thin veneer of English. Their island setting, coupled with proximity to the rest of Latin America, make it highly unlikely that Spanish will become secondary to English in the foreseeable future.

Spanish culture lingers on, too, in the choices and forms of Puerto Rican names. It is customary to use two surnames, that of one's father and one's mother. The father's family name comes first and is always retained, while the mother's family name comes second and is sometimes dropped. Thus Luis Muñoz Marín may be called Luis Muñoz but never Luis Marín. Upon marrying, a woman usually drops her mother's family name to take her husband's name, derived from his father with a *de* before it. Thus Felisa Rincón Marrero became Felisa Rincón de Gautier when she married. This popular public figure served as the mayor of San Juan for many years. Carlos Romero Barceló, who was elected governor of Puerto Rico in 1976, is married to an American woman who was born Kate Donnelly and is now properly called Kate Donnelly de Romero.

Even the introduction of United States currency in 1898 did not succeed in eliminating the use of the old Spanish words for monetary units. The dollar is still often called a "peso," a half dollar "medio peso," and a quarter a "peseta." And in the countryside it is not unusual to hear a twenty-five-cent piece referred to as "dos reales" (two Spanish coins or two bits) and seventy-five cents as "seis reales" (six bits).

However, despite all these cultural holdouts, the American influences on the island are enormous and, in the area of business and commerce, they are overpowering. The transformation of Puerto Rico from a rural-agricultural society to an urban-industrial one took place with almost lightning speed, in the course of a couple of decades. Many islanders are still reeling from these changes, and Dr. Gerardo Navas, Director of the Graduate School of Planning of the University of Puerto Rico, attributes the high proportion of schizophrenics and other mentally disturbed individuals and the amount of violent personal crime on the island to the "social disintegration resulting from the inability of human beings to adapt to so much upheaval in their lives."

The Puerto Rican who commutes by car on clogged roads two hours or more each day between home and office, factory, or other job has made an irreversible break with the past. There is, in fact, no quiet semirural or small-town life to go back to, for the island is literally paved with roads serving sprawling municipalities, and due to land scarcity housing communities are built at ever-increasing distances from urban centers. One really senses the crowdedness of the 3,400-square-mile island. With its population at 3.4 million, Puerto Rico has an average density of over 1,000 persons per square mile. And the concentration is, of course, much higher around San Juan.

The island's coastal railroad line built in the 1890's and routed from San Juan to Mayagüez to Ponce was abandoned decades ago in response to United States pressures for highway travel over rail travel. Now developed into an avid market for the American-manufactured automobile, as well as some European and Japanese imports, Puerto Rico has over one million cars, about one for every three people. Excise taxes that bring the cost of a $6000 vehicle to $10,000 have not discouraged many Puerto Ricans.

The incidence of traffic accidents is high (some observers see the reckless driving habits as an expression of lost individualism or stifled *machismo*), and unsightly auto junkyards are a growing blight. Although the cost of gasoline is about 25 percent higher than on the United States mainland, bicycles, mopeds, and other less fuel-intensive, environment-polluting vehicles have attracted little interest. Cruising the main avenues at night in cars outfitted with (illegal) trumpet horns is a favorite pastime of youth.

During the lengthy San Juan bus strike of 1978, the city somehow survived, despite even heavier traffic jams, with private cars, taxis, and *públicos*. *Públicos* are taxilike vehicles for hire, usually used for intraisland travel. They have specific destinations, stop at fixed points, and take as many passengers as they have room for, charging each a flat rate for the journey.

In the acquisition of automobiles, home appliances, furniture, clothing, sports equipment, and many other goods, Puerto Ricans have been encouraged to imitate the consumption patterns and the

85

A *piragua* seller in Ponce, and children sipping
cocos frios at the kiosks near Luquillo Beach

materialism of the United States. Advertising pressures are strong and create a "have-it-now, pay-later" philosophy. As a result, Puerto Ricans make down payments eagerly despite their lower incomes and the higher cost of imports. Installment and credit buying have been so successfully transplanted to Puerto Rico, enriching both manufacturing and financing institutions, that the island is often referred to as a "mortgaged society."

Many of the food preferences of today's islanders have been shaped by American food technology and by intense name-brand advertising. The widespread acceptance of frozen vegetables, meats, fish, and TV dinners also reflects the large number of refrigerator-freezers in island homes. And packaged and processed foods, high in cost and abounding in chemical additives, crowd supermarket and subsequently kitchen shelves, just as they do in the United States.

Favorite refreshments of an earlier day are the *piragua*, a cone of shaved ice topped with a thick fruit syrup of tamarind or guava, tropical fruit juices, and *cocos fríos*—chilled coconuts, whose liquid is sipped through a straw. Today they are losing their appeal to synthetically flavored soft drinks and accompanying commercial snack foods. Ironically, Puerto Rican oranges rot on the trees while island families drink frozen, canned orange juice from Florida, and sun-ripened pineapples from the lush fields of Arecibo are spurned for canned pineapple slices from Hawaii.

Television sells toys as well as sugar-frosted breakfast cereals to young viewers. The island is an ideal market for American manufacturers of children's products and for all advertisers seeking to capture lifelong consumers by molding their preferences during the formative years. Puerto Rican families are much larger than those in the United States, and the greater part of the population is under twenty-five.

Since the 1950's, television watching has become one of the most popular forms of recreation. In the early years of the medium, many of the municipalities provided public television sets in the town plazas, where the people of the community could watch outdoors through the warm evenings.

Today nearly 95 percent of the island's families own their own sets, very often color TVs, and there is a wide range of offerings including Spanish-language *novelas* (soap operas for the most part), comedy programs, variety and game shows, news reports, and sporting events. In general, the quality of the island-originated programs is poor. There is little incentive for Puerto Rican producers to compete with or try to improve upon the plentiful and popular situation comedies, police-action dramas, animated cartoons, TV movies, and other imports from the United States, which are most often Spanish-dubbed and appear to be well-liked by the majority of viewers. There is one noncommercial television station that carries local and imported programs of higher quality, several by arrangement with the National Educational Television network in the United States. The latter are presented in English. Cable television is available and consists almost entirely of American-originated programs and movies, also presented in English.

Movie theaters in Puerto Rico show films from the United States (which are usually Spanish-subtitled) almost exclusively. First-run houses in San Juan and in modern, suburban shopping malls charge admission prices almost as high as those in New York City for single-feature presentations. Mexican and South American films and TV offerings find little chance for an audience in the face of North American entertainment marketing and publicity techniques. As all radio and television licensing remains in the hands of the Federal government, the United States exercises legal control as well of Puerto Rican broadcasting.

While life in Puerto Rico seems more and more to resemble that of the United States—certainly in the areas most influenced by the mass media—the island *has* managed to preserve and even to revive interest in its folklore and its arts. It also has created a cultural and recreational scene born out of its unique blend of experience.

The music and dance of the past are re-created by talented young people like the members of the Ballet Folklórico Puertorriqueño. The company's repertory includes a program of the late-nineteenth-century salon dances that were performed by the upper-class society that once attended soirées and balls at the governor's palace in Old

Soirée dances being performed by the Ballet Folklórico Puertorriqueño, and the lively *bomba* re-created by the Areyto Folkloric Ballet

San Juan. The European waltz, polka, and mazurka were transplanted for these occasions. But most popular as dance music and also as a song form was the *danza*, light and melodic and reminiscent of the airs of the Spanish zarzuela, or operetta.

The island had its own famous and very prolific composer of *danzas*, Juan Morel Campos (1857–1896). He is often referred to as "the Johann Strauss of Puerto Rico." Even the Puerto Rican anthem, "La Borinqueña," with music by Felix Astol and words by the poet Lola Rodríguez de Tío (1854–1924), is based on a *danza*.

The African origins of Puerto Rican dances are seen in the *bomba* and the *plena*. The *bomba* (a name that also applies to a large wood-and-skin drum) is a vigorous, largely improvised, highly rhythmic dance that is a feature of the July *fiesta patronal* at Loíza Aldea. It is also performed, as is the *plena,* by the Areyto Folkloric Ballet of Puerto Rico. The *plena*, sometimes called a "mulatto dance," is said to have originated in the black slums of Ponce.

Among the projects encouraged by the Institute of Puerto Rican Culture has been a renewed interest in the guitarlike *cuatro*, so named because in its early form it was a four-stringed instrument. It now has ten strings in five pairs of two. Other modifications of the *cuatro* also exist. They, along with the ukelele-sized *tiple*, are once again being crafted on the island, and *cuatro* concerts are becoming increasingly popular. Traditional song is being revived, too, par-

Two young *cuatro* players rehearsing for a concert
at the Dominican Convent

ticularly the melodic *jíbaro* airs characterized by the musical expression, "le-lo-lai."

In 1956, at the age of seventy-nine, the great cellist Pablo Casals retired to Puerto Rico, the birthplace of his mother. He lived there until his death in 1973. Largely through his efforts, the island soon became an international music center. In addition to the renowned Pablo Casals Festival, which has been held every June, Puerto Rico now has its own Conservatory of Music and Symphony Orchestra. The island has distinguished native musicians such as the internationally famous pianist Jesús María Sanromá and draws guest concert artists from all parts of the world. Similarly, the government-sponsored Ballets de San Juan and the island's several opera groups have attracted top-ranking guest artists.

While young Puerto Ricans, especially, respond enthusiastically to the imported American popular music of the day, there have been several island-born composers and performers who hold a special place in their affections. Among them are the much-loved composer of popular songs Rafael Hernández, who died in the mid-1960's, the singer Tito Rodríguez, whose recordings have remained favorites since his recent death, and the blind singer-guitarist José Feliciano.

Folk arts and crafts are displayed and sold at the Dominican Convent under the auspices of the Institute of Puerto Rican Culture. The Institute also approves the authenticity of the handworked articles offered for sale at the weekly Artisans' Market held at *El Centro,* the spacious new Convention Center flanked by two hotels in the Condado beach-and-tourist section of modern San Juan.

The artisans who gather here come from all over the island. Their wares include handwoven hammocks and other string and basketry articles, ceramics, leather goods, papier mâché products, jewelry, novelty items fashioned from bamboo, shells, coconuts, seeds, and feathers, *santos* carved out of wood, and musical instruments like *cuatros* and *tiples,* as well as maracas and *güiros,* percussion instruments made from dried gourds. The *güiro,* of Taino Indian origin, is an elongated shape, ridged along one side and rhythmically scraped with a forklike or comblike stick.

From the sixteenth to the eighteenth century, religious subjects dominated the formal arts of Puerto Rico. In the town of San Germán, exquisite carved and painted statues of the Virgin and the saints were created. The island's most prominent painter of religious scenes was José Campeche (1752–1809). The nineteenth century shift to secular interests is seen in the work of Francisco Oller (1833–1917), who portrayed familiar subjects in his gentle still lifes and nature studies.

Outstanding among the artists of the present century have been Ramón Frade (1875–1954), who immortalized the *jíbaro* in his painting, *El Pan Nuestro* (Our Bread), and the bright modernist, Rafael Tufiño (born 1922), whose work is typified in his *Maternidad*. Both these paintings, along with representative works of Campeche and Oller, hang in the Museum of Puerto Rican Art in Old San Juan.

At the Ponce Museum of Art, there is an impressive wing devoted to Puerto Rican artists. A handsome building designed by Edward

An exhibit of the religious statuary of San Germán, at the Museum of the University of Puerto Rico

Maternidad, a painting by the modernist Rafael Tufiño,
in the Museum of Puerto Rican Art

Durell Stone, the museum houses a wide-ranging collection of
European and American art. It was given to the city of Ponce by its
native son, the wealthy industrialist Luis Ferré, who served as governor of the island from 1969 to 1972.

In the field of graphic arts, Puerto Ricans have produced a large

One of the handsomely designed galleries in the
distinguished Ponce Museum of Art

and distinguished body of work. Many of the island's galleries and
museums exhibit artists who are outstanding in the creation of
posters and other illustrative designs for books, calendars, theatrical
events, and purely decorative purposes. Best known among them is
Lorenzo Homar (born 1913), who began his career in the 1930's and
has influenced many younger artists.

Considering the small size of the island, Puerto Rico has a remarkably full theater calendar the year round. In addition to
performances of music and dance, there is a lively interest in drama,
and presentations range from classic works, many from the Spanish
repertory, to contemporary plays by American writers performed
in Spanish. Among Puerto Rican playwrights, the most prominent
figure of the nineteenth century was Alejandro Tapia y Rivera
(1826–1882) for whom the Tapia Theater is named. Built in 1832
and many times renovated, the theater with its pleasant arcaded sidewalk café is located opposite the Plaza de Colón in Old San Juan.

Puerto Rican dramatists, like the distinguished Luis Llorens
Torres (1878–1944), have frequently been poets and essayists as well,
deeply involved with the island's history and its Caribbean culture.
The poetry of Luis Palés Matos (1898–1959) pays tribute to Puerto

Rico's black heritage. This singling out of the African strain is quite unusual, for sensitivity to it generally lies buried deep in the Puerto Rican consciousness, as a result of the island's extensive racial integration and sense of cultural "oneness." As is often the case in Latin America, Puerto Rico's poets have been political figures, and vice versa. Luis Muñoz Marín, rich in literary expression from his youth, has been fondly called by his countrymen *El Vate,* The Bard.

Puerto Rico's contemporary novelists and short-story writers often deal with social changes and conflicts, such as the shift from rural to urban life, the experiences of army service, and migration to the mainland. Foremost among these literary observers is the short-story writer, playwright, essayist, anthologist René Marqués (born 1919), whose theme is often the ambivalence and ensuing hardship of Puerto Rican life because of the island's "two flags, two anthems, two loyalties."

Luis Palés Matos, whose poetry celebrated the black heritage of
Puerto Ricans, depicted in a sculpture on the UPR Río Piedras campus

This dual citizenship is vividly demonstrated by a glance at Puerto Rico's calendar of official holidays, which are numerous because all United States holidays are observed along with those of Puerto Rican origin. Washington's Birthday, Memorial Day (stemming from the Civil War), Independence Day, Thanksgiving Day, and others are unrelated to the Puerto Rican past. Island holidays that intermingle with them are the birthdays of historical figures like Eugenio María de Hostos (January 11), José de Diego, a prominent autonomist of the late nineteenth century (April 16), Luis Muñoz Rivera (July 17), and José Celso Barbosa (July 27). Dr. Celso Barbosa was the founder, in 1900, of the island's pro-American and prostatehood Republican Party.

March 22 is Abolition of Slavery Day, July 25 is Puerto Rico's Commonwealth Constitution Day, September 24 commemorates El Grito de Lares, and November 19 is Discovery Day. Religious holidays are celebrated somewhat differently from the way they are in the United States. Good Friday is the most solemnly observed of the Easter holidays. Older women still maintain the custom of dressing in black or purple, the colors of mourning, and try to visit seven churches, symbolic of half of the fourteen Stations of the Cross. Businesses, government offices, and even public beaches are closed for the day.

Following the Spanish tradition, El Día de los Tres Reyes (Three Kings' Day) on January 6 was once the time for Christmas gift giving. This day, known as Epiphany in English, commemorates the visit of the Wise Men to the infant Jesus. On the evening before, children would set out boxes filled with grass for the horses of the Three Kings (the camels of the Holy Land were unknown in Puerto Rico). Next morning the grass would have vanished and been replaced by Christmas gifts.

The introduction of North American Christmas customs brought Santa Claus and evergreen trees to the tropics and extended the period of festivities to several weeks. Well in advance of Noche Buena (Christmas Eve), neighbors and friends come together in roving parties of celebrants, called *parrandas*, to make rounds of visits singing carols and playing the *cuatro, güiro*, and maracas. Children may ask for small gifts of money. Municipalities, churches, and families in their homes set up nativity scenes.

At midnight on Christmas Eve churchgoers attend the Misa del Gallo, "mass of the rooster," the early-morning herald of the birth of the Christ child. Afterward a rich meal of roast suckling pig, *pasteles*, and *coquito* (a tropical eggnog made with rum and coconut milk) is served. December 25 has now become a time for gift giving as well as January 6. In between, falls the New Year celebration. Merrymakers may get a midnight dousing when families fling water from their balconies to toss out the evil spirits as the new year begins.

While the attraction of warm, sunny beaches during the winter months is Puerto Rico's most powerful tourist lure, islanders have an old superstition about avoiding ocean bathing during months that have an "r" in them. Many, in fact, make their first visit to the beach on June 24, San Juan Bautista Day, on the eve of which it is considered good luck to take a dip in the sea at the stroke of midnight.

Spectacle and betting sports like cockfighting and horse racing are favorite recreational activities. With its small dimensions and limited pastureland, the island never adopted bullfighting. But cockfighting goes back to the early days of the Spanish occupation. The contests were banned for a time after the American takeover, but they continued illegally. Cockpits, or *galleras*, range from the air-conditioned, carpeted Coliseo Gallistico in the Isla Verde section of San Juan to dirt rings in country towns. Betting is frenzied as the two sharp-spurred birds are set against each other in a fight to the death.

Thoroughbred racing is held at the island's famous El Comandante track. Traditional to Puerto Rico, however, is the Sunday or fiesta-time show of the *paso fino* horse. This small, elegantly stepping animal, developed from an Arabian breed, was brought to Puerto Rico by the Spanish because of its exceptionally smooth saddle gait, so well suited to the narrow trails of the island's interior mountain terrain. The raising and training of *paso fino* (fine step) horses was a pastime of wealthy colonists. Today there is a network of Paso Fino associations around the island. An experienced rider on one of these dainty, arch-necked animals should be able to carry a full glass of water without spilling a drop.

Like bettors everywhere, Puerto Ricans keep buying lottery tickets, in the fervent hope that they will gain overnight riches. Now government-run, the lottery, along with cockfighting, was a banned activity in the early years of the American occupation of the island. Today an underground or illegal lottery known as *la bolita* flourishes alongside the government lottery. *La bolita* is highly popular in the barrios, where sellers of the "numbers game" tickets are known to the rest of the neighborhood and where buyers can be trusted not to turn them in to the police.

Many Puerto Rican men are passionately devoted to the game of dominoes. Older men may spend long afternoons in parks and plazas or on shady sidewalks at this pastime, while more active ones repair to a favorite club for a *viernes social,* or "social Friday" evening game. The stubbornly retained institution of the "husband's night out" has caused much marital friction, especially among younger couples.

Puerto Rican fans have eagerly accepted the imported sports of tennis and golf, boxing and baseball. And a number of island-born athletes have distinguished themselves in these activities and achieved international fame. The Hiram Bithorn Stadium in San Juan is named for the first Puerto Rican baseball player to qualify for a United States major league. The island has a professional minor league of its own.

There has been no public figure in recent years who has stirred the hearts of the Puerto Rican people as has Roberto Clemente. Born in a suburb of San Juan in 1934, this sensitive and somewhat introverted young man achieved fame as a major-league baseball star only to be tragically killed in an airplane crash on December 31, 1972, while ferrying relief supplies to earthquake victims in Nicaragua. His body was never recovered from the sea, but many monuments to his memory exist on the island, and he was the first

A San Juan monument to Roberto Clemente, a beloved popular
figure and a symbol of acheivement

Latin American to enter the National Baseball Hall of Fame at
Cooperstown, New York.

At the time of Roberto Clemente's death, public-school children
all over the island were asked to write poems and essays expressing
their feelings and thoughts about this lost hero. A fourth-grade

child in Mayagüez wrote: "Clemente was so great that the earth could not hold him; so he had to be buried in the sea."

It has been said that all cultures need their heroes. But perhaps some need them more urgently than others. Through the period of rapid social and economic change that began in the middle years of the century, Puerto Ricans have been searching almost desperately for the charismatic leader to follow Muñoz Marín. So far no one has filled his place. Meantime, the island's population has continued to be propelled forward—with an accompanying degree of disorientation and disappointment—in what Luis Ferré has so aptly tagged *la nueva vida,* "the new life."

·IV·
The New Life

With the implementation of Operation Bootstrap in the early 1950's, Puerto Rico entered a period of great economic promise. The island that had for half a century been called "the poorhouse of the Caribbean" was about to become a modern industrialized society. Among the factors that would contribute to this economic miracle were the change to commonwealth status, which would mean political stability for Puerto Rico and security for United States business investment, and the offering of corporate tax exemptions, both Federal and local. These tax exemptions, combined with the low cost of island labor, would generate vast corporate profits, making the island truly an "investor's paradise."

For Puerto Ricans, the establishment of mainland industries requiring large labor rolls would mean jobs for the landless farmers and the urban poor. Wages, although far lower than in the United States, would be higher than the mere pittances received by the sugar harvesters and other agricultural workers.

Incomes from nonfarming jobs in the past had not been much better. Gone now were the days of the 1920's with their cottage industries, women laboring at home at piecework embroidery, handkerchief making, and glove making, entire families engaged in rolling tobacco for cigars. Even the introduction in the 1930's of factories for the manufacture of glass, cardboard, clay products, and cement for domestic use had failed to bring much economic improvement.

The name Operation Bootstrap (first talked about in the late 1930's) was changed after World War II to Fomento, meaning "promotion" or "development." In English, the Puerto Rican government agency involved was called the Economic Development

Oil refineries and petrochemical plants on Puerto Rico's south coast

Administration. Whatever its name, it did indeed foment, or stir up, a remarkable social and economic revolution.

Between the early 1950's and the early 1970's, some 3,000 factories, mainly United States manufacturing operations, were opened on the island; per capita income rose from about $250 a year in 1950 to $1,800 a year in 1973; and Puerto Rico outstripped all of its Latin American neighbors in improved health, education, and housing, and in general public betterment. Even oil-rich Venezuela lagged behind in average personal income and in its average standard of living.

These decades of economic growth also saw the development of more sophisticated kinds of manufacturing. In the 1950's, the emphasis was on factories producing baby garments, lingerie, footwear, and textiles. Puerto Rico became known at that time as "the brassiere capital of the world." Soon added, however, were plants that manufactured metal products, machinery, and electrical goods. And in the late 1960's, heavy industries like the oil refineries and petrochemical installations of the south coast were established. Today the emphasis has shifted to electronic, medical, and scientific precision instruments, such as minicomputers and heart pacemakers, and to the manufacture of pharmaceuticals. As a result, the island has earned the title of "pill capital of the world."

Puerto Rico's labor skills are now highly refined, its wage scales have drawn much closer to those of the United States, its living standards are higher than ever, and yet a very strange thing has happened. Unemployment is officially reported at close to 20 percent (40 percent among people aged sixteen to twenty-four); nearly two-thirds of the population qualifies for United States Federal food stamps; and the onetime "poorhouse" has now become the principal "welfare state" of the Caribbean. Clearly, several things have gone wrong with the economic miracle wrought by Fomento. What are they?

A major problem inhibiting real progress for Puerto Rico is its overpopulation. From 1 million in 1900, the number of inhabitants has soared to 3.4 million. And this does not include the 1.7 to 2 million Puerto Ricans who are at any given time living off the island, principally on the United States' mainland. Without this escape valve, Puerto Rico's narrow, 100-mile-long strip of land would somehow have to accommodate over 5 million human beings.

Compared to the population densities of neighboring island countries like the Dominican Republic, Haiti, Cuba, and Jamaica (which together average fewer than 500 persons per square mile), Puerto Rico's density of 1,000 persons per square mile is truly alarming. Yet the Puerto Rican birthrate, while higher than that of the United States, is only about half that of the Dominican Republic.

Puerto Rico's low death rate—directly traceable to improved hygiene and the introduction of modern sanitary and medical facilities from the United States—is what has accounted for the high population-growth rate of the past half century. Interestingly, Puerto Rico's death rate is today even lower than that of the United States, its average life-span of seventy-two-plus is a fraction longer than that of the United States, and the island is reputed to have more octogenarians in proportion to its population than any place in the world.

103

At the same time, people under the age of twenty-five make up more than half the population, and this group has many child-bearing years ahead of it. About 30 percent of Puerto Ricans are, in fact, under the age of thirteen. While family-planning advice and birth-control devices are freely available, political parties have been reluctant to advocate openly a program aimed at reducing population growth. The issue is highly sensitive, not only because of the traditional opposition of the Roman Catholic church but because of Puerto Rican attitudes regarding children and family life. A key expression of *machismo* is the fathering of children. The families that are reducing their size in Puerto Rico today tend to be in the middle and upper economic brackets, while the poor continue to have a higher birthrate. And although a trend toward a lower population-growth rate has begun to appear, its effects will not be felt until well into the next century.

Additional pressure on the island's population is being caused by reverse migration, a growing trend since 1971. Between 40,000 and 50,000 Puerto Ricans a year (in excess of those leaving) are now returning to live on the island. And, as Puerto Rico has no authority or control over immigration, which rests with the United States Federal Government, it has also become home to many Cubans, Dominicans, and other Caribbean peoples seeking political havens or economic betterment. The Cuban community on the island numbers 50,000 to 60,000. Most Cuban exiles are well educated, highly qualified in a variety of skills and professions, and have been economically successful. Dominicans and British Virgin Islanders often immigrate to Puerto Rico illegally, the latter by way of the United States Virgin Islands. As these illegals are ineligible for food stamps they take low-paying menial jobs or go into domestic service, often filling a gap left by Puerto Ricans who can get by as well or better on public welfare.

The good-paying factory jobs that most unemployed Puerto Ricans would like to have are simply not available. For a current labor force of about 950,000, Fomento industries and others provide about 150,000 jobs at best. By far the largest number of employed persons—about 23 percent as compared to less than 16 percent in manufacturing—work in public administration jobs. The expansion of the Commonwealth's government payroll has reduced the slack in the employment picture but has brought a heavy financial burden, deep public indebtedness, and extremely high local income taxes for the emerging middle class.

Another cause of unemployment—added to that of a population growth that has outstripped Fomento's efforts to provide jobs—is the loss of labor-intensive industries, those requiring large numbers of workers. As Puerto Rico began to grow less food and depended more on imports, as the United States expanded its markets there for costly consumer goods (automobiles, color TVs, stereo sets, washing machines, microwave ovens, and numerous other manufactured items), the cost of living rose and higher wage scales had to be put into effect. Many of the textile and needle-trade factories with large payrolls, particularly those manufacturing lower-priced products, fled to Haiti and the Dominican Republic, Taiwan and South Korea, where consumer expectations were low and labor was cheap. The newer Puerto Rican industries have been capital-intensive rather than labor-intensive. The massive oil and petrochemical operations of the south coast, for example, employ a small labor force of about 6,000 in comparison to their costly capital installation and the high price of their product.

Another reason for the economic downturn in Puerto Rico is the world recession that began in 1974, following the sudden quadrupling of the price of oil. Because of the large amount of American business investment in Puerto Rico, the island's prosperity is tied to that of the United States. But Puerto Rico not only reflects conditions in the United States; because of its small size and high concentration of American business activity, it also behaves as a magnifying mirror in which economic problems and their effects are more intensely experienced. Lingering damage caused by the recession is seen, for example, in the 1978 failures of the Commonwealth Oil Refining Company (CORCO) and the Banco Credito, Puerto Rico's third largest bank.

High-rise condominiums, with some still-unsold apartments, on the San Juan shore at Isla Verde; in foreground are pool cabanas

The CORCO bankruptcy was a delayed casualty of the oil-price increase. In the late 1960's plans were afoot to develop a profitable oil-refining industry, plus a huge tanker port, in Puerto Rico. These plans were based on hopes of importing cheap crude oil from Venezuela. But not long after the coastal refineries went into operation, the 1973 oil embargo was imposed, and the world price of oil zoomed. The tanker port, fortunately, was never built, for it too would have been beset with financial difficulties.

The failure of the Banco Credito y Ahorro Ponceno was also related to the recession, which struck at the height of an ambitious construction program on the island. The bank had too many loans outstanding on condominiums and commercial buildings, in various stages of completion, for which there were no longer buyers or a rental market.

Today, almost everywhere along the island's principal arteries, gaunt gray concrete structures on rusted metal skeletons stand as mute testament to the building boom that busted. Construction was one of the industries whose employment was most seriously affected by the recession. Of the 80,000 Puerto Rican workers in construction jobs in early 1974, less than half were able to find jobs in the years that followed. By 1978, there had been a very slight upturn to just over 40,000 jobs.

Despite the attractions of Federal tax exemption, and of Commonwealth tax exemption for ten to seventeen years, with the possibility of renewal, Fomento-promoted operations have been slipping away from the island. Of the 3,000 businesses introduced, only about 1,800 remain in Puerto Rico at present and not a great many new ones are flocking there. Even though tax-free profits have been enormous, corporations have been frightened off by labor demands, shipping costs (of raw materials inbound to Puerto Rico and finished products outbound), the independence movement, terrorist bombings (particularly of banks and business on the mainland that have island affiliates), and by the Commonwealth's stagnant economy and huge public-spending debt.

Another possible source of discouragement was the plan initiated in 1978 by the prostatehood governor, Carlos Romero Barceló. In an effort to offset the high cost of maintaining power, transportation, and other public services upon which island businesses depend, it was determined that Commonwealth tax exemptions for American and foreign corporations should be gradually reduced from the current 100 percent, over a long-term period. By varying the allowable exemption according to the type of business, environment-polluting industries, for example, could be made to contribute their fair share in taxes, while service industries such as industrial maintenance and repair facilities, architectural consultants, computer services, or mail-order houses would be granted a larger tax exemption.

In view of the excessively high personal income-tax rates on the island (even higher in some cases than for equivalent wage earners in the United States who pay both local *and* Federal taxes), this plan seemed to make good sense. But the question was whether it might not have the effect of driving American businesses out. And, of course, should Puerto Rico ever become a state, such businesses would be faced with having to pay Federal taxes as well.

Not all Fomento-promoted businesses are American-owned. Jap-

107

The Caribe Hilton, the first of Puerto Rico's luxury hotels;
Fort San Jerónimo, completed in 1788, is in the foreground

anese and other foreign firms have opened subsidiaries in Puerto
Rico, for they have been able to enjoy the twin advantages of Commonwealth tax exemption and easy entry into the American market.
But these businesses are in the minority compared to the overwhelming number of American operations. There are also some
large Puerto Rican-owned businesses on the island. They account,
however, for only about 9 percent of the total net manufacturing
income. Principal among them are the breweries that produce
Puerto Rico's India- and Corona-brand beers, rum distilleries, pro-
cessors of fruits and other tropical food products, and commercial
bakers.

Americans who know Puerto Rico mainly as a tourist destination
may be surprised to learn that the island's income from tourism
holds a distant third place after manufacturing, which is first, and
construction, which is second, even in its depressed state. Tourism
is, however, Puerto Rico's most visible industry, and it has been
a highly profitable one. It was inaugurated in the early days of
Fomento, under its long-time director, Teodoro Moscoso, with the
building of the Caribe Hilton Hotel in 1949.

From a mere 65,000 visitors in 1950, the island played host to 1 million in 1970. And tourism reached a peak year in 1974, with an influx of 1.4 million visitors, most of them from the northeastern region of the United States. Between the late 1950's and 1965, rapid growth was stimulated, in part, by the break in relations between the United States and Cuba, as American tourists switched from that popular Caribbean resort of the pre-Castro era. Also, low-cost package tours to Europe had not yet begun to lure summer travelers across the Atlantic so that the island functioned as an all-year resort, almost as popular in July as it was in January.

The Condado beach-front area became a strip of glittering high-rise hotels, and these tourist meccas then expanded eastward along the San Juan coast to Isla Verde near the island's international airport. In addition to the large hotels, numerous guest houses opened, featuring moderate-priced accommodations and access to the beaches, almost all of which are available to the public without charge or restriction.

Starting in the latter half of the 1960's, however, growth became more seasonal and Puerto Rican vacations became more expensive. The change was due in part to labor demands, as the cost of living on the island rose. The 1974 recession hit hard at tourism, and a number of hotels were forced to close.

Currently tourism is experiencing an upturn, the most recent figures indicating nearly 1.5 million annually. Contributing factors have been the extremely harsh winters of 1976–1977 and 1977–1978, the weakness of the American dollar abroad, attractively priced winter tour packages, and discount rates of up to 50 percent at luxury hotels during the mid-April to mid-December "summer" season. Cruise-ship visitors now number 450,000 a year, as numerous ships dock at the active harbor in Old San Juan. Also, the Commonwealth's new Condado Convention Center (*El Centro*), operated by Hilton International, promises to attract trade and professional functions and to increase the already large number of people who travel to the island on business.

At present, 8,000 to 9,000 Puerto Ricans are directly employed in tourism. However, indirectly supplied services and products for

Cruise ships that bring numerous visitors to Puerto Rico
docked in the harbor at Old San Juan

the industry may involve ten times that many workers. In the 1960's
many hotels and restaurants received complaints about the attitudes
and performance of their employees, most of whom had been propelled from mountain farms and city slums into an environment
and type of work for which they were ill prepared. In an effort to
improve courtesy and competence, the Commonwealth government
has for some years now operated a hotel school at Barranquitas. And
the Puerto Rico Tourism Company, a government agency, has been
carrying out a program to instill pride of work in all tourism service
personnel.

Today's visitor to Puerto Rico has begun to learn that the island
has far more to offer than the "sun, sea, and sand" attractions of
most Caribbean islands, although they are abundantly available, too.
Away from the tourist enclaves of the San Juan area, there are still
many easily reached, unspoiled beaches on the west, south, and
east coasts. A string of *paradores* (inns) in both mountain and shore
locations offer a taste of regional country life at modest cost. In addition, there are the rich historical and cultural attractions to be found
in Old San Juan, San Germán, and at the Indian Ceremonial Ball

Park near Utuado, as well as the striking scenic attractions of the El Yunque Rain Forest, the Cordillera Central, the karst country, the Río Abajo State Forest, Phosphorescent Bay, and the offshore islands.

For tourists who are United States citizens, no passport or visa for Puerto Rico is needed, nor are there any formal entry requirements. United States currency and the United States postal system are used on the island. Water is safe to drink, standards of hygiene and sanitation are high, and there are no tropical diseases to worry about. At the same time, there is ample opportunity for exposure to a Latin culture that has many exotic features, giving the traveler the sense of being abroad while experiencing many of the reassurances and comforts of home.

Puerto Rico qualifies as an important destination for Americans who subscribe to the theory that one should "see America first." Other conscientious citizens, too, would find it beneficial to visit Puerto Rico and to spend a portion of their time there "out on the island." For one thing, the image obtained will be very different from that which is dispensed at home by newspapers and television

Approach to the concourse of the spacious new Condado Convention Center

"The Ponce sound," a sidewalk performance by a local group
entertaining near the leafy Plaza Degetau in the island's second city

news teams, pointing up terrorist bombings and Hispanic ghetto
violence. For another thing, should statehood—or independence—
one day become an issue for Congressional consideration, an in-
formed and responsible United States citizenry will have an important role to play in the decision its government makes.

In the days before tourism or Operation Bootstrap were dreamed
of, the mainstay of the Puerto Rican economy was, of course, agriculture. Today less than 5 percent of the labor force, only about
40,000 workers, are employed on the land, and 85 percent of the
island's foodstuffs are imported. The two main dietary staples, rice
and beans, are grown and processed in the United States. In addition, one-third of the locally consumed coffee is grown elsewhere,
and the tobacco industry is on the verge of disappearing entirely.

Almost all of these changes can be attributed to the Americanization of Puerto Rico. Industrialization through United States investment revamped the economy. No effort was made to apply the new
postwar farming technology to the island's agriculture. And express
efforts were made to build a market for United States food exports
in Puerto Rico. Even Muñoz Marín was swept up in the rush to-

ward industrialization and ready to turn his back on farming. True, as Muñoz aptly phrased it, the agriculture of the past had been devoted largely to producing "the after-dinner pleasures without the meal."

He was referring, of course, to sugar, coffee, and tobacco, the cash crops of a colonial possession designed to supply the mother country with luxuries from the tropics, which either could not be grown at home or could be grown in its colonies more cheaply and abundantly. In Puerto Rico especially, land that might have been devoted to producing meals for the island's population was taken over for sugarcane cultivation during the first half century of Americanization.

Today sugar production, which reached a peak of 1.3 million tons in 1952, is down to 250,000 tons a year. And the number of working sugar mills on the island has steadily decreased from forty in 1943 to twenty-five in 1952 and to seven at present. In the lowlands once devoted to cane growing, the tall brick chimneys of abandoned

The seventeenth-century Porta Coeli Chapel in the main plaza of the historic town of San Germán

A working sugar mill near Auada, one of the seven *centrales*
still active on the island

centrales, smokeless against the sky, are a common sight. And they
may soon be joined by some of the more modern working mills, for
in 1978 raw sugar cost twenty-six cents a pound to produce in
Puerto Rico and sold on the world market for twelve or thirteen
cents a pound. The difference was made up through a government
subsidy. Most of the cane lands and all of the mills are owned by
the Commonwealth's Sugar Corporation. Small farmers did receive
some of the acreage of the big American sugar corporations after
Muñoz Marín had them parceled out through the enforcement of
the 500-acre law. But because of their outmoded farming practices
and lack of financial resources, few made a success of cane growing
and the land parcels were eventually bought up by the Commonwealth government.

Sugarcane growing is unprofitable in Puerto Rico today for several reasons. The coastal lands, where mechanical reaping can be employed, have to a large extent become urbanized or given over to industrial development. Much of the island's cane is grown on sloping terrain and must be hand cut, a method that is slow and inefficient as well as expensive because of Puerto Rico's high labor costs (far exceeding those of most of the world's sugar-growing areas). At present, some 12,000 workers are seasonally employed in the fields and in the mills. Many are older workers, for few young men are lured to the soil despite high unemployment rates.

Although several distilleries still manufacture rum in Puerto Rico, they are holdovers from an earlier era when the island actually had a sugar surplus. Today more than half the molasses used in rum distilling comes from off the island, principally from the Dominican Republic. In addition, most distillers bottle only a small proportion of their product in Puerto Rico. Because of high labor and shipping costs, most of the rum that leaves the island does so in bulk containers for bottling elsewhere. The Bacardi Distillery, for example,

The bottling plant of the Bacardi Rum Distillery at Cataño

maintains a relatively small bottling plant at Cataño across the bay from Old San Juan, but it finds it more profitable to do most of its bottling on the United States mainland, its principal market. This policy has, of course, meant a loss of jobs among the island's rum-distillery workers.

Distillers explain that rum is relatively expensive to produce because of the aging process required, and so the industry must pare its costs in order to keep prices competitive with those of other alcoholic beverages popular with American consumers. The major steps in rum-production are fermentation, distilling, and aging. The first takes place in enormous vats filled with molasses, water, and yeast. In the distilling stage, after fermentation, the alcoholic content is developed and the impurities are filtered out. Lastly comes aging, in charred-oak casks, which takes one year for white rum, three years for amber rum, and six years for *añejo*, a special, deep-flavored dark rum.

Islanders have long been making *cañita*, a bootleg rum, for home and local consumption. *Cañita* was in wide demand during the era of American Prohibition (1919–1933), for this ban on the sale of alcoholic beverages was also imposed on Puerto Rico. Another popular cane product on the island is *guarapo*, or sugarcane juice, usually sold chilled at roadside stands.

Unlike cane growing, coffee growing remained in the hands of small farmers and hacienda owners after the American takeover. Traditionally cultivated in the shade of banana and citrus trees on steeply sloping mountain farms, the island's coffee bushes were so severely damaged by the hurricanes of 1899 and 1928 that coffee production has never really recovered. Puerto Rico today produces some twenty-six million pounds of coffee a year compared to the fifty million it was producing just prior to 1928. The island's agricultural experts are enthusiastic about a new method of coffee-growing, with full sunlight, which offers a much higher yield per acre. Although several such plantings are now under way, production has far to go to meet even local needs.

Tobacco growing in Puerto Rico has declined steadily over the

116

years. A 1977 drought drastically cut the harvest of this now-minor crop, and in that same year the island's largest tobacco-processing plant closed.

The cultivation of "after-dinner pleasures" may well have seen its day in Puerto Rico. But the growing of rice and beans, fruits and vegetables, and tubers like the *yautía* and the *batata*, as steps toward self-sufficiency in food, certainly seems a worthwhile goal. The island has a year-round growing climate, a variety of usable soils, and excellent water resources both for natural and for artificial irrigation.

Rice and beans could yield two crops yearly as opposed to one in the United States. Citrus fruits, mangos, avocados, and a number of other tropical and subtropical fruits could be grown in abundance for island consumption, as could all sorts of vegetables. It is astonishing that at present even the *yautía* and the *batata* are supplemented with imports from the Dominican Republic; that supermarkets and roadside *colmaditos* alike offer apples from Washington state, pears from Oregon, and oranges from Florida; that restaurants and hotels serve salads made with iceberg lettuce grown in California and Arizona, while island farmers stand by the side of the road offering flavorful, tender leaf lettuce fresh from the fields.

Irregular production, semiabandoned or poorly cultivated farmlands, outmoded technology, and the lack of an effective marketing system are all responsible to a degree for the dependence and vulnerability of the Puerto Rican food supply. But even more serious impediments to self-sufficiency have been government policies and the American economic grip on Puerto Rico.

A glaring example of misdirected government policy is the subsidizing of the dying sugar industry. The monies spent over many years might have helped farmers grow a variety of foods for local use. Only recently have funds begun to be turned to that purpose. With them the Commonwealth is hoping to develop modern, diverse small farms of about 200 acres each on former cane lands through both agricultural rentals and purchase loans.

Admirable as these beginning efforts are, there is a second prob-

117

lem. It is questionable whether the American food industry can be made to withdraw from the profitable market it has carved out in Puerto Rico. In fact, many island consumers accustomed to United States products and pressured by the media to continue to buy them may well refuse to give up their jarred baby foods, canned peaches in heavy syrup, and squash-proof tomatoes picked green and crated in Texas for long-distance shipment. Conditioning by commercial interests is strong, and consumer education has yet to gain a foothold in Puerto Rico.

The massive reeducation of young people toward an appreciation of the new farming and an understanding of its goals is another hurdle. But, if successful, it will produce numerous benefits including a sharp drop in unemployment, for most island crop production, even with modern technology, would be quite labor-intensive.

The attempt to establish dairy, beef, pork, poultry, and egg production in Puerto Rico has met with limited success. Livestock, feeds, and equipment have all had to be imported from the United States, making local products more expensive than the frozen beef, chicken, turkey, and pork shipped from the mainland. And even at a similar price, not many islanders prefer the *carne del país*, "meat of the country" that comes from the butchering of either old milch cows or young bull calves of the dairy-industry herds.

The Puerto Rican dairy industry has been the most successful of the newer ventures. However, a quart of island-produced milk is more expensive than milk in the United States and is lower in fat content. Dairymen point out that cows produce less milk in the tropics and that the better milch breeds are very costly. Through established preference, many housewives still use canned milk and many schools buy powdered milk for their lunch programs. Both products are American imports.

In a recent attempt to develop a new agricultural export, Puerto Rico has established an ornamental-plant industry. These exotic plants, which can be cultivated in the moist, tropical mountain regions without greenhouse expense, have so far found a favorable market in the United States. But, in a world that hovers frighteningly close to a global food shortage every few years and in which food has become an international bargaining tool on a par with petroleum, the growing of edibles in this ideal island environment is what seems of primary importance.

How is "the new life" working out on a day-to-day basis in this modern, industrialized society? In view of the high cost of living in Puerto Rico, one of the most puzzling questions is how its people can manage to survive on an average per capita income of about $2,500 a year (less than 40 percent of the United States average of over $6,000). The answer is that they cannot.

In order to prevent a return to the abysmal poverty and neglect of the 1930's, and in order to keep islanders buying the over two billion dollars' worth of consumer goods imported annually from the United States, the Federal government spends several billions a year on a variety of programs for Puerto Rico. Not the least of these is the over $800 million a year now being expended for food stamps. Food stores everywhere, both large and small, display the

A butcher's stall in the Río Piedras farmers' market; its sign announcing *carnes del país* also states that food stamps are accepted

sign: *Aceptamos cupones para alimentos.* (We accept food stamps.) The use of food stamps by nearly two-thirds of the island's population frees money for other purchases and keeps the economy humming deceptively well by means of artificial props.

The cost of the food-stamp program and other welfare measures is not borne by the Federal-tax-exempt American businesses that reap large profits from their operation in Puerto Rico. Nor is it borne by Puerto Rican citizens who, because they lack representation in the Federal government, are exempt from Federal taxation. It is borne by the taxpayers of the United States, who are, in effect, supporting American business both on and off the island so that a small, overpopulated Caribbean isle can remain the United States' sixth largest export market in the world.

Because most things on the island cost about 15 percent more than they do on the mainland, Puerto Rican wages have been rising, and the gap between island and mainland salaries has been narrowing. At the start of Operation Bootstrap, the average Puerto Rican wage in manufacturing was about one-third of that in the United States; today it is up to between one-half and two-thirds. Fomento wage scales are generally above the United States minimum wage and are Federally established and frequently reviewed. Nevertheless, the family of a Puerto Rican worker earning $6,000 or $7,000 a year often qualifies for food stamps, especially if there are a large number of dependents, because of the island's severe inflation, which is much higher than on the mainland.

At present, considering the island's recession-caused slump and ensuing economic stagnation, there seems little hope for a meaningful increase in personal incomes. In the early decades of the century, Puerto Rico had a strong labor movement under the leadership of Santiago Iglesias Pantín. But its solidarity was shattered during the independence troubles of the 1930's and by the death of Iglesias Pantín in 1940. Today strikes by public employees, like those of the electrical workers and the San Juan bus drivers in 1978, are looked upon unfavorably by much of the public as well as by the debt-ridden Commonwealth administration. In private industry, labor's hands are also pretty well tied, for a manufacturer with labor troubles is likely to pack up and shift operations to a Caribbean or Asian location that is more inviting. Social-security and unemployment-insurance programs operate in Puerto Rico, but certain features of social-security insurance such as aid to the blind, the elderly, and the disabled have been covered, in the past, under another Federal program.

Although the island does have a growing middle class, there is still a very uneven distribution of wealth in Puerto Rico. Some ten or twelve island families are reputed to control vast interests in real estate, finance, retail trade, and other enterprises. A notch or two below them on the economic scale are the wealthy professionals and businessmen who live in the exclusive residential enclaves of San Patricio and Santa María. Although part of metropolitan San Juan, these secluded neighborhoods have gracefully curving streets with luxurious Mediterranean or ranch-style houses set on spacious landscaped grounds.

But on a small, crowded island the homes of the wealthy are never very far from the slums and public housing of the very poor or from the *urbanizaciones* and condominiums of the lower-middle

A run-down street in Old San Juan, the island's
first center of urban life

Dwellings of the historic slum of La Perla, nestled between
the city wall and the sea

to upper-middle classes. The jumble and variety of housing in San
Juan and its surrounding municipalities is a reflection of the way
in which city living has developed on the island. This phenomenon
began in 1521 with the building of Old San Juan and exploded in
the twentieth century until it extended well beyond that historic
center.

As old as Old San Juan is the *arrabel*, or slum, of La Perla, a
strip of beach front not far from El Morro that was left unprotected
when the city wall was built. Seen from the road just above the
wall, the houses tumble down on six or seven levels from the heights
to the sea. Several decades ago, during the early years of the rural-
to-urban shift, 8,000 to 9,000 people were compressed into La Perla
living in indescribable squalor. In the mid-1960's, anthropologist
Oscar Lewis made La Perla the subject of his famous study, *La Vida*,
(thinly disguising the notorious slum as La Esmeralda). At the time,
it was a warren of squatters' shacks, some of which stood on stilts
on the beach in constant danger of being washed away by heavy
seas.

Today many inhabitants have been moved into public-housing
projects, and the population is estimated at 3,000 to 4,000. Many of
the houses now have green tar-paper roofs donated by the city,

painted-board exteriors, and are fairly large and substantial looking, although within they are parceled up into family living quarters that are entered from different street levels. A few concrete-walled buildings have appeared, although such "permanent" construction is forbidden by law on land taken over by squatter communities.

There is still crime, vice, and an active drug traffic in La Perla, which is entered through one of several narrow passageways carved out of the thick Spanish city wall, and the outsider is likely to be surveyed with some wariness and suspicion. But living there also are working-class families whose members have jobs on the nearby San Juan docks and in various municipal service agencies. Above all, this historic Puerto Rican slum in its seafront setting appears to be a community with a strong sense of solidarity and a lively neighborliness.

Less well-known but far more ugly, dirty, and depressed are the squatter settlements along the muddy Martin Peña Channel, a sluggish stream that meanders its way for four and a quarter miles from an inland lagoon out to San Juan Bay. One of these settlements has been fittingly named El Fanguito (from *fango* meaning "mud" or "slime"), while another is glowingly known as Buena Vista. Some 40,000 to 50,000 people live directly along the banks and, lacking sanitation services, dump garbage and sewage into the channel, where they mingle with industrial wastes.

The Martin Peña communities grew up between the two world wars and soared to over 70,000 in population as the dispossessed farmers and poverty-ridden sugar workers streamed toward the city in those preindustrial years. The inhabitants are still among the poorest in San Juan. Today the Martin Peña slums are gradually being reduced as alternate housing is provided. And a plan is being studied to drain the channel eventually, relocate all its squatters, and develop it into a much-needed transportation artery.

The first public-housing projects for the poor, begun in the late 1950's, were the *caseríos*, blocks of three- and four-story concrete buildings with running water, indoor toilets, electricity, kitchen sinks and stoves, built-in closets, and other modern conveniences.

A unit of a new *caserío* at Dorado, its street wall decorated
with a mural painted by a local artist

Despite these attractions, many slum dwellers were reluctant to
leave their old neighborhoods. The new apartments were cold looking, with empty, boxlike rooms that demanded furnishings the
occupants could not afford. The sameness of the buildings caused
confusion and offered no sense of identity.

The new neighborhoods had broad, impersonal streets with heavy
motor traffic instead of the narrow, intimate lanes of the slums, and
the supermarkets would not extend credit as had the small neighborhood *colmados*. Nor did personal values improve markedly.
Much of the poor hygiene and squalid housekeeping moved right
along into the *caseríos*. And, as priests, social workers, and city
officials affirm, the drug-dealing and other illicit activities seemed
to concentrate even more strongly and involve more of the residents
in the *caseríos* than in the slums. Relocation into *caseríos* has continued, however, and the newer ones appear more attractive and
better maintained.

For families slightly above the poverty level, private developers
offered *parcelas* in the years between the wars and immediately
following World War II. They were small plots of land, usually
improved with water, sewers, and electricity, offered for sale at
minimum cost. The buyers could then have a reasonably priced
"shell" house built, which they finished and improved themselves.

Advertising a new urban housing development outside Humacao,
"800 down; low monthly payments," and some of the recently completed
houses

Parcela houses seen nowadays generally have corrugated iron roofs
and wooden or concrete exteriors. They are highly individualized
in color and exterior features, and almost all have *rejas*, iron grill-
work enclosing porches and other open areas, as both decoration
and protection against vandalism and burglary. *Parcela* developments tend to provide their own neighborhood services, as corner

125

houses are turned into grocery stores, bars, driving schools, and small churches.

As most *urbanizaciones* of the postwar era have been built in outlying districts, carports are a distinctive feature of the housing units. The automobile is an essential link between home and one's place of employment, as well as the shopping center in which most of the community services are concentrated. A typical tract house in a Puerto Rican *urbanización* closely resembles a minimum-standard six-room ranch house in the United States. Its three bedrooms, one or two bathrooms, living room, dining room, and kitchen areas are tightly arranged and constructed with materials of basic quality. Owners frequently enclose their carports to provide extra living space for growing families. As each house extends almost to the limits of its building lot, windows tend to look into other windows, and there is little privacy.

Building sites for *urbanizaciones* are now reaching to the outskirts of San Juan satellite municipalities such as Bayamón. With a population already well over 150,000, it is possible that Bayamón, to the west of San Juan, and even Carolina, which lies to the east, may soon outstrip Ponce as the island's largest population areas after the capital. As metropolitan San Juan itself is now home to over one million, virtually only high-rise housing is being constructed there, either new public developments for limited-income families or the luxury-type "condos" built by private investors.

Family life in San Juan has come to resemble that in any large city on the United States mainland. Unlike the countryside, where several generations may still live clustered together under one roof, the city offers only compact apartments or houses built on small lots with little room for expansion. Often the family with a great many children will send some off to the countryside, on a revolving basis, to stay with grandparents or other relatives.

An enduring feature of Latin-American life, as in many other cultures, is the designation of godparents, an institution known as *compadrazgo*. The *comadre* (comother) or *compadre* (cofather) takes on a long-term affectionate and protective role toward the godchild

126

and has a lifelong, binding friendship with the child's parents as well. In the past, the child's *madrina* (godmother) or *padrino* (godfather) was often selected from among acquaintances of some wealth and prestige to ensure a stand-in parent in the event of an emergency. Today many family services are supplied by social-welfare agencies, but the godparent institution lingers on and has many pleasant and warming aspects. Who else but a loving and conscientious godfather would undertake to round up twelve of his godchildren, ranging in age from five to thirteen, and escort them to the circus in San Juan?

Although women have played a subservient role in most Latin cultures, Puerto Rican society has strong matriarchal traditions that seem to have carried through from Taino and *jíbaro* patterns into present-day urban life. Women of the lower socioeconomic classes, especially, often show enterprise and independence in carrying the entire responsibility for the family. According to Oscar Lewis and other social observers, many such women actually prefer a consensual union to legal marriage because they can end the former more easily if it is unsatisfactory. Experience has taught the women of the poorer barrios to be wary of the man whose *machismo* is threatened by economic hardship, for he will often vent his resentment against society on his wife and children.

The Puerto Rican woman of the middle and upper classes may find herself caught between older and newer life-styles. She may have a job or career, drive her own car, work in her spare time for a charitable organization or even a political party. But her husband may still insist on his "social Friday" privileges, deny her an equivalent "night-out-with-no-questions-asked," no matter how innocent, and refuse to help with household chores. However, a recent series of conferences on women and the family reveal that male attitudes are slowly changing. Even though the Puerto Rican man may consider himself too *macho* to do the dishes, he is apparently learning to recognize woman's need for personal fulfillment and to accommodate to it.

Women have long made up a substantial portion of the island's

Young women in the small mountain town of Las Marías (pop. 7000), who may have a promising future on their rapidly changing island

labor force. More women than men worked in the cottage industries of the 1920's, and the factories of the 1930's drew large numbers out of their homes for the first time. Over half the workers in Fomento industries are women, and the unemployment rate for women is lower than that for men. The difference is due, in part, to the preponderance of jobs in light manufacturing on the island and, in part, to the family responsibilities many women carry alone. Women also have a history of political participation in Puerto Rico and were numbered among· the revolutionary leaders at Lares in 1868.

In the professional and political jobs traditionally held by men, Puerto Rican women have begun to make a modest but respectable showing. There have been women on the Commonwealth's supreme court, in the island's Senate and House of Representatives, in the governor's cabinet, and serving as mayors of several Puerto Rican cities and towns. Most famous of them is Felisa Rincón de Gautier, who was mayor of San Juan from 1946 to 1968. Dr. Belén Serra, the woman who as Dean of Studies at the University of Puerto Rico at Río Piedras is second in command to the Chancellor, says of women's growing participation: "Puerto Rico can be viewed as a small laboratory. It has undergone rapid social change and is open to further change. Things can and do move more quickly here."

Rapid social change is also reflected in the island's health picture. Formerly, those illnesses related to unhygienic living conditions and lack of sanitation were among the leading diseases. They included dengue fever, schistosomiasis, elephantiasis, hookworm and other intestinal parasites, skin diseases, tuberculosis, and tetanus. Today these diseases have fallen off dramatically, and the once widespread yellow fever and malaria have been completely wiped out. Now increasingly prevalent among Puerto Ricans are cancer and cardiac-pulmonary diseases. Interestingly, they are major health problems in the United States, and their rising incidence appears to be related to the fact that so many Puerto Ricans are now eating a diet high in animal fats, living and working amidst industrial and other pollutants, and experiencing the anxieties and tensions of urban life.

Among communicable diseases, syphilis and gonorrhea are the most prevalent. Alcoholism and drug addiction are extremely serious problems. And schizophrenia and other psychotic conditions afflict a higher percentage of armed-forces veterans from Puerto Rico than from any state in the Union. All of the foregoing are, of course, symptoms of a pressured society that has been required to make a major and rapid social and economic readjustment.

Public-health care is about 75 percent Commonwealth-funded and is provided in the form of clinics, hospitals, and health centers. The ratio of doctors to inhabitants is more than twice as high as in the Dominican Republic, for example. But it is far from adequate. Due to understaffing and heavy case loads, clinic health care is not always satisfactory. Those who can afford to patronize private physicians and hospitals do so, or they travel to the mainland for treatment.

Another heavy financial burden for the Commonwealth government is education, on which it now spends close to 30 percent of its annual budget. Most of this expenditure goes toward paying teachers' salaries. Requests for increased Federal funding for edu-

cation frequently meet with congressional opposition on the ground
that islanders do not pay Federal taxes. The exceptional difficulty
in educating Puerto Rican youth stems in large part from the am-
biguous political status of the island. Yet that same ambiguity is
impeding efforts to improve the situation.

Because commonwealth status does not clearly define the national-
ity of Puerto Ricans (and because statehood and independence both
are possibilities for the future), an effective educational program
must at present straddle both worlds, that of the Hispanic Caribbean and that of the United States. Island children need to be
taught to read and write Spanish and to use that language as a tool
for studying mathematics, science, social science, and other subjects.
At the same time, they must study English as a second language,
beginning with vocabulary in first grade and giving it the same
emphasis as Spanish from second grade on. And they must ingest,
in whatever language they can, American history, geography, government, public affairs, and current events.

This task is beyond the capacity of the system. Puerto Rico's
schools are run-down and poorly equipped. Teachers, most of whom
are women, are inadequately trained for their complex bilingual
work, and classes number forty to fifty students. In addition, the
past several years have seen an influx of some 30,000 children from
reverse-migrant families into the public-school system. Most of
these newcomers were born in the barrios of New York and other
mainland cities. Their families have returned to Puerto Rico hoping for an assimilation into society that was denied them in the
United States. School authorities report that, in general, the neo-
Rican children (born of Puerto Rican parents in the United States)
are non-Spanish-speaking. Alien to island culture and toughened
by big-city life, they tend to be aggressive and disruptive, sometimes
impairing class discipline and inhibiting learning as they once again
seek an identity that eludes them.

Although public education is free and compulsory, the Commonwealth government estimates that about 7 percent of Puerto Rican
children aged six to twelve are not enrolled in school at all. And

of the children who do attend school, about half do not complete more than seven years of the twelve-year system (which is divided into six years of elementary school and three years each of junior and senior high school). Encouragements like free lunches, free rural transport, small cash subsidies, and cut-rate urban transport have helped to keep most students in school through the sixth grade and to raise the literacy rate to over 90 percent. But the difficulty of mastering enough English to perform well in the upper grades appears to be a discouraging factor that leads to dropping out. Only about one-third of Puerto Rico's total population are high-school graduates. This proportion includes the 12 percent of the island's youth that attends private schools.

Pupils in Puerto Rican public schools must wear school uniforms, each school choosing its own. These uniforms serve to blur the distinction between richer and poorer children and, at the same time, to identify the student who may be tempted to wander off school grounds when he or she should be attending classes.

The University of Puerto Rico, the island's public institution of higher education, originated at the turn of the century as a school for the training of teachers. It was officially designated a university in 1903 and has since expanded greatly on its parklike Río Piedras campus at San Juan. The UPR's Mayagüez campus was established in 1911 as the home of the College of Agriculture and Mechanical Arts. Mayagüez today has 9,500 students, Río Piedras has 24,000 full-time students (60 percent women), and the total UPR enrollment, including the Medical Sciences campus, regional colleges, and adult and noncredit enrollees, comes to about 50,000.

There are also several private universities on the island. Principal among them are Inter-American University, with campuses at San Germán and also in San Juan's Hato Rey district, and Catholic University at Ponce. Altogether Puerto Rico has about 120,000 students attending schools of higher education, not including those students at universities in the United States and elsewhere.

What careers are open to the university graduates of such a small and overcrowded island? Chancellor Ismael Rodríguez Bou of the

Students of the Río Piedras campus in the entry court
of the Museum of the University of Puerto Rico

Río Piedras campus admits that the UPR appears to be educating
its students for jobs that do not exist. "But the idea," he says, "is
to get them educated and then let their capabilities fulfill themselves." And indeed, with Puerto Rico functioning as a cultural and
economic link between the United States and the Hispanic world,
many of the island's graduates in business administration, science,
and technology are eagerly snapped up by the countries of South
America.

The UPR has had its share of student activism, reflecting both
local educational problems and wider political issues. There have
been demands for curriculum reform, more classes taught in Spanish, fewer required texts in English, and a more open admissions
program. Today there is a liberalized admissions formula, with 20
percent of the freshman class accepted on the basis of academic
potential and/or artistic or other special talent rather than proven
academic standing. And the UPR tuition is only about ninety dollars per semester.

The Río Piedras campus, in particular, has been the scene of an
active proindependence movement and of protests against the draft-
ing of Puerto Ricans for the war in Vietnam. Riots in the late
1960's and early 1970's resulted in the banishment of the United

States armed forces' Reserve Officers Training Corps from the campus. At Mayagüez, however, there is still a functioning ROTC unit. University authorities attribute its survival to the conservative, unpoliticized atmosphere of the smaller west-coast campus, where most students are involved in agriculture and applied sciences and there are fewer courses in the social sciences and the humanities. Aside from a small, visible radical political group, the Río Piedras campus has been very quiet, too, for some years, and the political views or tendencies of most of the student body are difficult to assess. Nowadays a loudspeaker on campus is as likely to signify a meeting of a revivalist religious group as a political rally.

While the educated, bilingual Puerto Rican can go abroad for a career and often return to the island to play a distinguished role in its academic, economic, or political life, the poorly educated Spanish-speaking Puerto Rican, leaving the island in search of wider opportunity, finds that his or her disadvantages tend to follow along.

As American citizens, Puerto Ricans can, of course, travel freely to or from any part of the United States. Spurred by a booming mainland economy and a swelling island population, migration became a major phenomenon of the postwar years. Prior to World War II, the number of Puerto Ricans residing in the United States had grown slowly, from about 12,000 in 1920 to 70,000 in 1940. Then, between 1945 and 1964, 750,000 people left—one-third of the island's population. By the late 1970's, there were about two million United States residents of Puerto Rican origin, including children born in the United States of Puerto Rican parents. One million were concentrated in New York City and environs, with others living in Chicago, Hartford, Detroit, Miami, and scattered in smaller communities throughout every state, including Alaska and Hawaii.

The job-seeking islanders who came north to harvest crops, perform menial, low-skilled services as hotel, restaurant, and custodial workers, or even to exercise their skills in the needle trades, in factories, crafts, and clerical positions were quickly stereotyped by other American citizens on the basis of their speech, appearance, and low economic status. Although a small proportion has moved into the middle class, this ethnic group as a whole has remained at the bottom of the social and economic scale. Nearly 28 percent of Puerto Rican families living in the United States fall below the Federal poverty level and are welfare recipients. Economically, they have been held back by a low educational level, lack of facility in English, and the stigma of being a lately arrived immigrant group with many dark-skinned members. Ghetto-type housing and substandard schooling and working conditions are further limitations imposed on these victims of social and racial prejudice.

As the Puerto Rican surge to the mainland was motivated by the search for jobs, there have always been small reverse flows of migrants back to Puerto Rico during periods of minor business recession. That pattern has accelerated since the major recession of 1974, and today there are more Puerto Ricans returning to the island each year than are leaving it.

A major problem of adjustment faces the long-absent Puerto Rican or the neo-Rican, who is shocked and dismayed to find that blending in with island life is difficult. In addition to being spurned for his or her poor or nonexistent Spanish, for brash, ungracious attitudes acquired on the mainland, and for insensitivity to the island's culture and mores, the reverse migrant also finds that island living is far more expensive than anticipated, that housing is scarce, and that San Juan feels even less like home than New York did. Alien to both cultures, incapable of being fully integrated into either one, the returned Puerto Rican is truly caught between two worlds.

One distinct advantage, of course, of living in the United States is that, once local residency requirements are established, the Puerto Rican citizen can vote in Federal as well as state and local elections. With the island-dwelling population denied a voice in the United States Congress, one would think that a strong political consciousness would develop among migrated Puerto Ricans on behalf of those back home who have no vote. Yet, while mainland-based advocates of commonwealth, statehood, and independence have established small, local followings, this pattern does not seem to have occurred on a noteworthy scale. New York's Puerto Rican community *has* produced Herman Badillo (born in Caguas, Puerto Rico in 1929), who served as Bronx borough president in the late 1960's, was elected to Congress in 1970 to serve for three and a half terms, and became deputy mayor of New York City in 1978. And it has produced other significant political and community leaders of Puerto Rican origin. But the concerns of Puerto Rican residents in the United States have been tied, justifiably, to numerous immediate problems of housing, jobs, education, discriminatory practices, and the like. And, aside from sporadic terrorist acts, there has been little activism regarding the issue of the island's political status or other difficulties plaguing the Commonwealth.

Should the trend toward reverse migration continue, possibly the prostatehood element on the island will be strengthened. Many neo-Ricans feel strongly committed to the United States despite the social prejudice and limited economic opportunity they may have encountered there, and they do not share the deep emotional involvement of the pro-commonwealthers and the *independentistas* in the preservation of the island's centuries-old culture.

Meantime, Puerto Rico's economic and social problems remain complicated by its political uncertainty. Policies, programs, and administrators have been changing every four years as the commonwealthers and the statehooders have tended to alternate gubernatorial stints in La Fortaleza, while those favoring independence argue from the sidelines that nationhood is the only road to self-fulfillment for the Puerto Rican people.

·V·

Commonwealth, State, or Nation?

"Neither, my friends, is there any room on this island for any flag other than the Stars and Stripes. So long as Old Glory waves over the United States, it will continue to wave over Puerto Rico."

With these words, spoken in 1921, E. Montgomery Reily, who had just been appointed governor of Puerto Rico by the president of the United States, expressed the confidence and complacency with which colonialism was viewed during the first half of the twentieth century.

Thirty years later, with the onset of commonwealth status, Puerto Rico was permitted to hoist its own single-starred flag and to fly it alongside that of the United States. But the real meaning of the paired flags has always been open to question, and the increasingly complex economic and social problems of recent years have placed that question in ever sharper focus.

Independents, of course, have always wanted to see the Puerto Rican flag fly alone; statehooders have already redesigned the white-and-blue panel of the United States flag into an arrangement that holds fifty-one stars; while commonwealthers cling defensively to a dual-flag status that, despite its flaws, seems to have worked for three decades.

The structure of the present Commonwealth government is based on the island's constitution adopted in 1952, which is, in turn, closely modeled on the constitution of the United States in its separation of executive, legal, and judicial powers, its guarantees of civil and human rights, and its other features designed to preserve the democratic process.

The island's governor is popularly elected by all citizens over the age of eighteen (reduced in 1970 from age twenty-one) and serves for four years with no limit on the number of reelections. He or she must have resided in Puerto Rico for five years prior to election and must be a United States citizen and at least thirty-five years old. The governor appoints a cabinet, and as there is no lieutenant governor, the secretary of state takes over should the governor not be able to complete the term in office. Owing to the small size of the island, the chief executive has fairly direct control of all public departments such as education, public works, commerce, agriculture, social services, labor, the treasury, and so forth. Political patronage is an acknowledged fact of Puerto Rican life, and party affiliation and loyalty are primary requirements for appointment to key positions.

El Capitolio, the gleaming white capitol building with its tall, classic entry columns and cupola-topped dome, is the seat of the island's legislature—its Senate of twenty-seven members and its House of Representatives of fifty-one members. Both houses are popularly elected, and their members serve four-year terms. As salaries are relatively low, most legislators maintain law careers or hold other professional or business positions, and much of the legislation is introduced by the executive branch. The governor can veto legislation, but the legislature can override the governor's veto with

El Capitolio, the seat of the island's two-house legislature

a two-thirds majority vote. Legislators are expected to be bilingual, but Spanish is the working language, both oral and written, of both houses.

Puerto Rico has a system of district courts, superior courts, and a supreme court for the highest decisions on matters of island jurisdiction. But should a question involve the Federal government, it could be taken for final appeal to the United States Supreme Court. Mayors are now elected by popular vote, although formerly the mayor of San Juan was appointed by the municipal assembly. Following the retirement of Felisa Rincón de Gautier in 1968, Carlos Romero Barceló served two elected terms as mayor before going on to the governorship as a result of the 1976 elections.

Islanders take their voting very seriously, and the turnout in gubernatorial elections has been consistently well over 80 percent, as compared with turnouts of between 50 and 60 percent of all eligible Americans in recent United States presidential elections. Symbols like the *pava*, the wide-brimmed straw hat, of the PDP and the *palma*, or coconut palm, of the NPP help to sort out the parties for those with limited literacy. There is a local residency requirement of one year for voting, so a non-Puerto Rican American citizen living on the island is able to participate in an island election. Corrupt practices in the early years of voting have led to a painstaking system whereby all the voters of a given district must arrive at their polling place at a given time. The doors are then locked and voting proceeds until all registered voters have cast their ballots. No longer does anyone have an opportunity to vote twice on election day.

The Commonwealth's tax revenues come largely from personal-income taxes and real-estate taxes on island residents and from excise taxes on a number of items, including automobiles. Federal taxes collected on rum bottled and sold in Puerto Rico are turned back to the Commonwealth treasury. But with almost no taxes derived from manufacturing, which brings in 43 percent of the island's total net income, Puerto Rico is highly dependent on assistance from Federal sources for funding all sorts of essential public operations and services. One might say that what the United States

Jaime Benítez, former University of Puerto Rico
president and United States Resident Commissioner,
and a prominent commonwealth supporter

takes away from Puerto Rico via its untaxed businesses and its rent-
free military bases, it paternalistically gives back in the form of wel-
fare-state generosity.

Even commonwealthers, who were the architects and are still the
staunch supporters of the current system, admit to its imperfections
and want, in the words of former Resident Commissioner Jaime
Benítez, an "improved commonwealth." Benítez, who served in
Washington from 1972 to 1976, has long tried to have the language
of Public Law 600, which was passed in 1950, changed because of
the following sentence: "The provisions of this Act shall apply to
the Island of Puerto Rico and to the adjacent islands belonging
to the United States, and waters of those islands." The word *belonging* is offensive because it implies ownership and smacks of colonialism, a violation of the "free associated state" concept.

And there are also a number of operative features in the relationship with the United States that commonwealthers would like to
see modified. Jaime Benítez, a distinguished professor of the University of Puerto Rico, who served as its chancellor for twenty-three
years and president for five years prior to his term as United States
Resident Commissioner, points among other things to the lack of a
structured channel of communications between the representative
of the people of Puerto Rico and the White House.

In general, American presidents have not expressed their prefer-

139

ence on the issue of the island's status. An exception was Gerald Ford, who on December 31, 1976, twenty days before leaving office, declared he would submit legislation to Congress to admit Puerto Rico as a state. President Ford's lame-duck gesture was apparently designed to appease statehooders, who have traditionally allied themselves with the Republican Party of the United States. But this empty pledge was high-handed, as well as meaningless, for only 48 percent of the island's voters had put the statehood gubernatorial candidate into office in the election of November, 1976. This vote did not constitute a mandate for statehood, and the president showed no concern for the wishes of the other 52 percent of the Puerto Rican people.

Another growing sore point expressed by commonwealthers is the island's lack of control over immigration. More and more displaced Latin Americans gravitate to Puerto Rico, either directly or by way of the United States mainland. Despite their talents and contributions, they add to the ever-increasing population pressure.

On the related issue of unemployment, the island's greatest problem, many commonwealthers would like to see a reform in Federal welfare legislation that would replace the food-stamp giveaway with work projects, which are sorely needed. The difficulty in initiating these and similar changes is again due to the lack of an effective avenue of approach to Washington's lawmakers.

How do commonwealthers feel about the obligations of citizenship, including the military draft that has required disenfranchised islanders to serve in United States wars? Between World War I and the Vietnam War, more Puerto Ricans, proportionate to the population, lost their lives serving in the armed forces than did citizens from any of the fifty states. This high percentage may well have reflected the use of Puerto Ricans in unusually dangerous actions and/or their limited understanding of military orders given in English.

Commonwealthers tend to be exceptionally loyal American citizens, grateful for the protection of their own island by United States military forces, especially during World War II, and they have for the most part accepted the military draft and the United States naval operations on the offshore islands. In connection with military and other installations, the Federal government has the right of eminent domain, whereby it can force Puerto Ricans to sell any lands required for public use.

Commonwealthers do feel, however, that Puerto Rico should have a right to protest an obligation of citizenship that it regards as undesirable or hostile and that Federal legislation not properly applicable to Puerto Rico should be subject to review by a joint commission. But built-in legal barriers and United States' indifference have so far thwarted attempts to "perfect" the commonwealth status or to dignify the relationship by giving Puerto Rico a more participatory role in what is now an admittedly one-sided compact.

The defeat, in 1976, of Rafael Hernández Colón, the procommonwealth governor seeking a second term, was in large part a reflection of the island's economic difficulties following the 1974 recession. Also there was no question that the procommonwealth PDP, which had been supported by approximately 60 percent of the voters from the 1950's through the 1967 plebiscite, had been losing popularity as the economic boom began to play itself out and as commonwealth status was held up to closer scrutiny. In the election of 1972, Hernández Colón had come to power with only 51 percent of the vote, despite strong support from the party's father figure, Luis Muñoz Marín.

Critics of the commonwealth relationship see it as having, at best, outlived its usefulness as a step in the island's evolution toward a more clearly defined status, either statehood or independence. They cite the failure of so influential a figure as Muñoz Marín to get Congress to consider creating a body such as a Bureau of Puerto Rican Affairs in the Department of State or of the Interior. Sharper critics have attacked Operation Bootstrap, asserting that Puerto Rico has become an economic vassal of the United States as a result of the commonwealth relationship. In any case, Puerto Rico today obviously reflects the economic and social policies of the United States, fostering big-business development on the one hand and an extensive public-welfare system on the other.

What is the real strength of Puerto Rico's anticommonwealth groups, the *estadistas* (statehooders) and the *independentistas*? It is difficult to know because voting counts at election time do not tell the whole story. For example, radically autonomist commonwealthers might at any point ally themselves with independents to prevent the stateholders from gaining strength, or conservative commonwealthers might ally themselves with statehooders for fear of seeing the island go independent.

The goal of statehood can be traced back to the formation in 1900, by Dr. José Celso Barbosa, of the Republican Party, which favored close cooperation with the American authorities. But the colonial exploitation of the island soon shattered dreams of early admission to the Union. Support increased in the plebiscite of 1967, with prostatehood elements registering 38.98 percent of the vote, and in the 1968 gubernatorial victory of Luis Ferré, with 44 percent of the vote. Ferré's New Progressive Party, the NPP, was a direct outgrowth of the old Republican Party. Its 1968 victory was due, however, to a split in the ranks of the PDP. The NPP again polled 44 percent of the vote in 1972, but lost that year to the unified Populares.

Statehooders were jubilant in 1976 when the NPP took 48 percent of the vote against 45 percent for the PDP. They saw a long-awaited turning of the tide. The new governor, Carlos Romero Barceló, promised to improve the island's economy before asking for a plebiscite to measure the number of Puerto Rican voters favoring statehood. But like his predecessor he was relatively powerless to deal with far-reaching problems like unemployment, declining business investment, a huge public debt, and social disintegration. He soon began to press more urgently for statehood as a means of treating the island's difficulties and, at the same time, granting to Puerto Ricans the right of full citizenship.

As a state of the Union, Puerto Rico would become entitled to substantially more Federal aid than it is now receiving. Its citizens would also be able to vote in Federal elections and would be represented in Congress with two senators and probably seven representatives, based on the size of the island's population at the time. Puerto

Carlos Romero Barceló, elected governer of Puerto Rico
in 1976 on the prostatehood ticket

Rico would probably have a larger numerical vote in the House
and in the electoral college than about half of the other fifty
states.

As inhabitants of the fifty-first state, Puerto Ricans would, of
course, have to pay Federal taxes. But, as statehooders argue, personal-income taxes are already extremely high on the island and
could actually be lowered with more funds coming from the Federal
government. With Puerto Rico a state, United States business would
no longer enjoy Federal tax exemption there. Still, statehood spokes-
persons assert that there are a number of factors that would keep
industry in Puerto Rico: just as states vary in their rates of taxation,
at least partial island tax exemption could continue for some time;
the island has a well-qualified, highly skilled and sophisticated labor
force; the excellent year-round climate precludes loss of production time due to winter storms; and Japanese and other foreign
companies would continue to find Puerto Rico attractive because
of partial tax exemption and its proximity to the mainland market.

During the Luis Ferré administration of 1969–1972, the NPP
governor talked of *"jíbaro* statehood" to allay fears of Puerto

Ricans that they would have to give up their Hispanic culture upon joining the Union. Governor Carlos Romero spoke even more determinedly on this issue, highlighting the assets of a Spanish fifty-first state, one that would "help the Nation bridge the gap of misunderstanding with Latin America."

Possibly Congress's acceptance of Puerto Rico as a state would indeed be interpreted as an act of respect and equal regard for a people of Latin-American culture and would improve relations with Mexico and countries of Central and South America. And the admission of a Spanish-speaking state would not introduce an entirely new cultural element into American life. Already the mainland Hispanic population, particularly in the southeast, the southwest, and the large cities of the north, is increasing so rapidly—reflecting immigration from many parts of Latin America—that Hispanics are expected soon to outnumber the nation's black population. It seems likely, too, especially in view of Puerto Rico's physical isolation, that elements of Spanish culture, consistent with the ongoing Americanization process, would be retained on the island.

Statehooders also point out that two noncontiguous states—Alaska and Hawaii—were admitted to the Union as long ago as 1959. They feel that the already strong ties to the United States—through industrial development, mainland cultural and consumer influences, the migration process, and tourism—have made Puerto Rico more "American" than either of the other two were at the time of their admission and hence more ready for statehood. And they contend, above all, that democracy cannot function without a representative form of government and that the rights of 3.4 million people who are now second-class American citizens must be recognized.

Despite these persuasive arguments for statehood, commonwealthers are not swayed. They retain a commitment to the "separateness" of Puerto Rico, a conviction that the "interdependence" of the commonwealth arrangement is a sensible and practical reality that offers Puerto Rico the best of both worlds, and a faith that, further developed, the Estado Libre Asociado would become, in the words of Jaime Benítez, "mutually enriching and uplifting. Then," says the island's former representative in Washington, "the ugly duckling will have turned into a swan."

No matter what dedicated and passionate beliefs Puerto Ricans may hold, changes or modifications in the island's status require legislation in the United States Congress. What are the chances that Washington would be receptive to a bid for statehood?

One of the most frequently cited arguments against the island's admission is the cost to the American taxpayer. In 1977, the average per capita income of Puerto Rico was $2,472, about half that of Mississippi, now the poorest state in the Union. Unemployment on the island is at least three times higher than the United States average. And the drug addiction rate is believed to exceed that of New York City. The prospect of higher Federal taxes, both personal and corporate, to support this new social and economic burden would be all too likely to evoke public antipathy to the measure.

Another problem is that of lingering ethnic, racial, and religious prejudice in American society. Although minorities won considerable redress and recognition through the civil rights activities of the 1960's, it would be unrealistic to deny that bias still exists. In any case, a large voting bloc of over five million (including the two million Puerto Ricans residing on the mainland) might be viewed by other Americans as too powerful a "special-interest" group, one with a Latin culture, African racial strains, and a predominantly Roman Catholic religion.

Conditions surrounding the 1959 admissions of Alaska and Hawaii were quite different from those of Puerto Rico today. In Alaska, the Eskimo and Indian groups were considerably outnumbered by a Caucasian population whose culture blended with that of the other forty-eight states. The territory was enormously rich in natural resources and was militarily and strategically valuable because of its proximity to the Soviet Union. In Hawaii, the Pacific peoples were economically and politically dominated by resident Americans with extensive agricultural interests and the islands themselves were a Pacific outpost of proven worth. Even so both territories had to petition many times before statehood was granted.

In Puerto Rico, the resident Anglo-American population is small, perhaps 50,000 to 60,000, and the aeronautic capabilities and long-range missiles of modern warfare have considerably reduced the island's military value.

But of far greater consequence is the problem of divided sentiment regarding statehood among the Puerto Rican people themselves. How high a plebiscite vote in favor of statehood would be considered adequate to guarantee Congress a new state without a permanently unhappy and potentially secessionist or terrorist population—60 percent; 75 percent; 90 percent? Examples of Britain's Northern Ireland, Canada's Quebec Province, and Spain's Basque region, with their inflamed separatist minority groups, are all too vivid.

Puerto Rico itself is so advanced in the operation of democracy, governing an electorate with such a broad spectrum of political thought and activity, that the island would quite possibly have to revert to an absolutist form of government before a wholehearted assimilation into the Union could be assured. Some political observers have even suggested that Puerto Rico would have to accept an interim status as a territory, with a United States-appointed governor, for a time. How else could the election of a procommonwealth or even a proindependence governor be prevented following the submission of a petition for statehood?

The island's democratic experience and representative form of government, plus its history as a nonrevolutionary society, are indeed unique in the Latin-American world. So entrenched, in fact, is the democratic system that islanders' widespread fears of an independent Puerto Rico going communist like Cuba or giving rise to repressive dictatorships like those of Haiti or the Dominican Republic in recent decades are very likely misplaced. In the words of Rubén Berríos Martínez, president of the PIP (Puerto Rican Indepence Party), "Puerto Rico is far more ready for a democratic form of government as an independent nation than the United States was at the time it obtained its independence from England." And, of course, slavery and other very serious inequities did exist in the young American democracy. Independents also point out that the excolonial Caribbean countries and the newly emerged African nations that have fallen far short of democratic achievement are poor examples for comparison with Puerto Rico, for their societies were rooted in feudalism or other forms of authoritarianism at the time of independence.

The PIP, which was formed in 1946, had been preceded in its bid for island independence by the activist Nationalist Party of Pedro Albizu Campos. The PIP approach to change, however, has been civil-political, and, in 1952, the year the commonwealth constitution was adopted, those advocating independence were the second most powerful group on the island, after the commonwealthers, with an election vote of 19 percent. Statehooders lagged behind with less than 13 percent at that time.

Commonwealth status, however, appeared to satisfy the political goals of the autonomists, while Operation Bootstrap and migration to the mainland offered unprecedented economic opportunities, and so the independence vote dropped off considerably in the late 1950's and the 1960's. In 1968, independence supporters registered an election vote of only 3 percent. The count has since begun to creep upward slowly, with just under 5 percent in 1972 and around 6 percent in 1976.

While these figures may not seem significant, students of the political scene are aware of the strong potential of the independence movement. There is believed to be a concealed support of at least 15 to 20 percent among commonwealthers. And, if the threat of statehood grew, many more commonwealthers with strong separatist convictions might declare themselves for independence. Interestingly, even statehooders might opt for independence. After a 1978 visit to the United States, Governor Carlos Romero Barceló declared that if a petition for statehood was rejected, he would favor independence for Puerto Rico.

Independence advocates have always felt that sovereignty is the only acceptable status for Puerto Rico, that national identity is not compatible with either statehood or commonwealth. And there is growing support for independence from the new middle-income class of government workers and retail and office employees. Labor

147

unions, university staff members, student groups, intellectuals, and people involved in the arts have long formed the basis of the movement.

On the other hand, people in lower-income groups, the urban and rural poor who are by and large food-stamp and welfare recipients, have not thrown themselves behind the independence cause. Apparently lulled into indifference by the Federally funded handout system, they seem to lack a long-range political awareness and, in the view of social and political observers, to respond mainly to election-time promises, supporting the candidate who seems likely to obtain the most public benefits for them. Pointing to this group, *independentistas* see the American presence in Puerto Rico as having brought demoralization, turned the island into a charity case, sapped the dignity and self-respect of working people, and induced rapid social deterioration as evidenced by high rates of drug abuse, alcoholism, crime, and broken families.

In the United Nations, charges of colonialism have frequently been leveled against the United States, particularly by the seventy-five or so former colonies that have emerged as nations since World War II. Each year the U.N.'s Committee on Decolonization hears testimony from Puerto Rican independence leaders asserting that their island is one of the last remaining colonies in the world.

"How," asks PIP leader Rubén Berríos, who is a graduate of Yale Law School and Oxford University and a former UPR law professor, "can a country that battled for its own independence, that professes democracy and the recognition of human rights, deny Puerto Ricans theirs? Why should Puerto Rico have to struggle with the United States for the very principles that are those of the United States?"

The strongest pressures from the United States for Puerto Rican independence will come, say advocates of the island's sovereignty, when American taxpayers understand that keeping Puerto Rico in assistance monies is costing them two to three billion dollars a year. The purpose of this contribution from taxpayers' pockets is to bolster the island's economy artificially so that American corporations can continue to do what they cannot do in the United States:

Rubén Berríos Martínez, president of the Puerto Rican Independence Party, which is drawing growing support from Puerto Rico's middle class

avoid paying Federal taxes. From the Puerto Rican side, according to the PIP, islanders must come to understand that nationhood does not mean either political revolution or economic disaster.

Already the Puerto Rican environment is strained and blighted by the expansion of industry. Instead of further industrialization, Berríos sees the development of a diversity of small- and medium-sized businesses and agricultural operations for Puerto Rico. He foresees that consumption patterns of Puerto Ricans will have to be scaled down, particularly for large, gas-guzzling automobiles and other imported luxury and optional goods. On the other hand, the transition to a more self-sufficient economy, one that is realistic and practical for Puerto Rico, need not be abrupt.

Both American and foreign-owned businesses might well wish to continue operating there, for large corporations have amply demonstrated—with subsidiaries all over the world—that they know no flag in their pursuit of a return on their investments. As an example, the Dominican Republic is seeing the establishment of more and more United States business ventures, despite a history of military dictatorship and political instability. "But," Berríos points

149

out, "an independent Puerto Rico must have the right to accept or reject such foreign investment; it must not have an imposed economy."

Nor would Puerto Rico as a nation have to sever other ties with the United States. Naval bases could remain there, as they do in other foreign countries. But the United States would naturally be required to pay rent, which they do not do now. Monies for development programs would have to be sought from international-assistance agencies, rather than from the United States exclusively. Some financial aid might come from the oil-exporting nation of Venezuela, which looks favorably on independence for Puerto Rico.

With the loss of United States citizenship, migration to the mainland would be a formal immigration process, and some Puerto Ricans would choose to leave the island permanently. And tourism would possibly fall off for a while. But PIP supporters maintain that an independent Puerto Rico, set on the path to self-determination and economic stability with the encouragement and goodwill of the United States, would be a showcase nation, an example to Latin American and other nations of all that is best in both worlds.

Nonetheless, many Puerto Ricans are fearful of going the route of independence. They are alarmed by the leftist threats of the small but radical PSP (Partido Socialista Puertorriqueño, or Puerto Rican Socialist Party) and of the terrorism of the F.A.L.N. (Fuerzas Armadas de Liberación Nacional, or Armed Forces of National Liberation).

The Puerto Rican Socialist Party was founded in 1971 by Juan Marí Bras. Mayagüez-born, Marí Bras is a Marxist, who advocates independence for Puerto Rico under a Marxist-Leninist system but promises a Puerto Rican communism that will be neither Russian nor Cuban. In the 1976 election, the PSP polled 0.7 percent of the vote. But it has been highly visible, displaying its red and black colors and slogans, and has been considered responsible for sabotage activities during strikes by government utility and transport workers.

The F.A.L.N. appeared on the scene in 1974, the most recent in a succession of terrorist fringe groups that have small and shifting

Juan Marí Bras, leader of the Puerto Rican Socialist Party, speaking before the United Nations Committee on Decolonization

bases of operation and have been difficult to track down or to link with any of the island's political parties. Most of the members of the F.A.L.N. appear to be young people, often neo-Ricans, who have been radicalized on the mainland. In order to dramatize their protest against "yanky imperialism," they have carried out close to seventy bombing attacks. Their principal targets have been United States Government and corporate offices in New York, Washington, Chicago, and Newark. Most serious was the January, 1975, bombing of Fraunces Tavern, a historic restaurant in New York City's financial district, in which four people were killed and fifty-three injured. In two 1977 bombing incidents of midtown New York office buildings, one person was killed. And, in 1978, a series of minor explosions were set off at major airports in the target cities.

Barbarous as these senseless attacks against innocent people are, it does not necessarily follow that the cause of independence is itself a bad one. Independence advocates point out that terrorism is to be found today just about everywhere in the world and that extremists exist on the fringes of almost any movement.

From the point of view of the United States, the principal drawbacks to Puerto Rican independence would probably be economic

151

"Death to yanky imperialism!!"; a message scrawled
on the wall of a building in Old San Juan

and strategic. Industry would object to the loss of a tax-free manufacturing haven and to the loss or reduction of a profitable market
in which to sell its capital equipment and consumer goods. It might
also balk at giving up the unexploited copper resources of the island.

Military strategists would surely bring up the issue of Cuba as a
Soviet satellite and recommend that the United States presence in
Puerto Rico be maintained as an ideological bulwark against Russian influence in the Caribbean. Some members of Congress might
also argue that the narrowly approved Panama Canal Treaty of
1978, arranging for the relinquishment of the American-built canal
to Panama in the year 2,000, constituted enough of a "giveaway" in
the Caribbean.

On the other hand, the high cost of maintaining Puerto Rico as
a commonwealh, the economic downturn on the island, and the
pressures from the United Nations and from all advocates of self-
determination might well bring the prospect of independence closer.
If nationhood for Puerto Rico did come to be looked on more
favorably by the United States, rather than as a somewhat disloyal

152

and subversive view, possibly many more Puerto Ricans would be encouraged to express their feelings.

At present, however, most of the political ferment on the island is not directly concerned with independence but revolves around the struggle for power between statehooders and commonwealthers. Following the approach used by Luis Muñoz Rivera in 1897 to obtain the Charter of Autonomy from Spain, some of the island's political leaders have tried to obtain support for their programs from the two major political parties in the United States. The traditional alliances have been statehooders (the NPP) with the Republican Party and commonwealthers (the PDP) with the Democratic Party.

A closer affiliation with United States political parties became possible in 1972 when the United States Supreme Court recognized the right of the citizens of Puerto Rico to send delegates to stateside party conventions to vote for presidential nominees. This expression of choice, within a national-party framework, is not the same, of course, as direct participation in national public elections, from which islanders remain barred. Some PDP members, however, immediately registered their opposition to voting at a United States political convention on the ground that doing so would be a step toward "assimilation."

The 1976 elections, in which the NPP polled more votes than the PDP, intensified the struggle between the two over the question. As the Democratic Party had attained power in the United States in 1976, with the election of the Democratic candidate for president, the NPP began to cross traditional party lines in order to press the ruling Democrats for statehood and planned to send delegates to the party's 1980 presidential convention.

In response to this threat, one faction of the PDP proposed that a group of island delegates be sent to the United States to counter NPP influence in the Democratic Party. At the same time, other PDP members held to the staunchly autonomist point of view and continued to oppose *any* participation in United States party politics. And to add a truly jarring note to the growing factionalism of the

Rubén Berríos, president of the Puerto Rican Independence Party,
at the United Nations, making a statement on behalf of Puerto Rican
nationhood

island's politics, still other PDP members declared themselves to be
prostatehood and formed a new political organization, which they
called the New Democratic Party.

In the future, the conventions of major political parties in the
United States promise to produce lively contention within the
PDP, as well as between the PDP and the NPP, while independence
advocates carefully assess the scene for their opportunity to pick up
additional support.

Puerto Rican newspapers report the almost daily power plays and
maneuverings within the island parties and have an eager readership.
Among the principal Spanish-language papers are *El Mundo*, which
is procommonwealth, *El Nuevo Día,* which is prostatehood, and
Claridad, which is proindependence. But, as elsewhere in the world,
a headline-shrieking newspaper is the one that has captured the
largest circulation. It is *El Vocero,* and its accent is on crime and
sensationalism. The English-language *San Juan Star,* which is read
by the American community and by many bilingual Puerto Ricans,
offers a balanced coverage of island news and United States news.
Only a single page is devoted to news of the Virgin Islands and the

rest of the Caribbean, reflecting the strong focus of the island on the North American nation with which it is so closely linked.

No one can speak with certainty about Puerto Rico's future political status. A national defense emergency for the United States or the discovery of oil in the island's offshore waters, for example, might advance the possibility of statehood, as might any number of unknown factors. Other unforeseeable events might spark the issue of independence, bringing it much closer than it now appears to be. Will there one day be a fifty-first state known as Puerto Rico? Will there perhaps be a small Caribbean nation known as the Republic of Boriquén? Almost anything can happen, and quickly, in our world of fast-moving developments.

For the present, however, commonwealth status seems most likely to continue. Many would say that this likelihood is not necessarily because of its virtues but rather for lack of a more acceptable means of striking a balance between two worlds.

Bibliography

Aitkin, Thomas, Jr., *Poet in the Fortress: The Story of Luis Muñoz Marín*. New York: New American Library, 1964.

Crampsey, Robert A., *Puerto Rico*. Harrisburg, Pa.: Stackpole Books, 1973.

Farr, Kenneth R., *Historical Dictionary of Puerto Rico and the U.S. Virgin Islands*. Metuchen, N.J.: Scarecrow Press, 1973.

Hauberg, Clifford A., *Puerto Rico and the Puerto Ricans*. New York: Hippocrene Books, 1974.

Lewis, Oscar, *La Vida: A Puerto Rican Family in the Culture of Poverty—San Juan and New York*. New York: Random, 1965.

Mintz, Sidney W., *Worker in the Cane: A Puerto Rican Life History*. New Haven: Yale University Press, 1960.

Negrón de Montilla, Aída, *Americanization in Puerto Rico and the Public-School System 1900-1930*. San Juan: Editorial Universitaria (University of Puerto Rico Press), 1971.

Steiner, Stan, *The Islands: The Worlds of the Puerto Ricans*. New York: Harper and Row, 1974.

Tugwell, Rexford G., *The Stricken Land: The Story of Puerto Rico*. New York: Doubleday, 1947.

Wagenheim, Kal, *Puerto Rico: A Profile*. New York: Praeger Publishers, Second Edition, 1975.

Wagenheim, Kal with Wagenheim, Olga Jiménez de, Editors, *The Puerto Ricans: A Documentary History*. New York: Praeger Publishers, 1973.

Index

ABOUT THE AUTHOR

Lila Perl was born and educated in New York City, and she holds a B.A. degree from Brooklyn College. In addition, she has taken graduate work at Teachers College, Columbia University, and at the School of Education, New York University. She is the author of a number of books for adults and for children, both fiction and non-fiction. Several of them concern life in other lands. In preparation for writing them, Miss Perl travels extensively in the country, doing firsthand research and taking many photographs. Her husband, Charles Yerkow, is also a writer, and they live in Beechhurst, New York.